VIRTUE ETHICS IN CHRISTIAN PERSPECTIVE

CASCADE COMPANIONS

The Christian theological tradition provides an embarrassment of riches: from Scripture to modern scholarship, we are blessed with a vast and complex theological inheritance. And yet this feast of traditional riches is too frequently inaccessible to the general reader.

The Cascade Companions series addresses the challenge by publishing books that combine academic rigor with broad appeal and readability. They aim to introduce nonspecialist readers to that vital storehouse of authors, documents, themes, histories, arguments, and movements that comprise this heritage with brief yet compelling volumes.

RECENT TITLES IN THIS SERIES:

Cascade Companion to Evil by Charles Taliaferro
Metaphysics by Donald Wallenfang
Phenomenology by Donald Wallenfang
Virtue by Olli-Pekka Vainio
Reading Paul by Michael Gorman
The Rule of Faith by Everett Ferguson
The Second-Century Apologists by Alvyn Pettersen
Origen by Ronald E. Heine
Athanasius of Alexandria by Lois Farag
Practicing Lament by Rebekah Eklund
Forgiveness: A Theology by Anthony Bash
Called to Attraction: The Theology of Beauty by Brendan T. Sammon
A Primer in Ecotheology by Celia Deane-Drummond
Postmodern Theology by Carl Raschke
Jacques Ellul by Jacob E. Van Vleet and Jacob M. Rollinson
Understanding Pannenberg by Anthony C. Thiselton
The Becoming of God: Process Theology by Ronald Faber
Theology and Science Fiction by James F. McGrath
The U.S. Immigration Crisis by Miguel de la Torre
Feminism and Christianity by Caryn Riswold
Queer Theology by Linn Marie Tonstad

VIRTUE ETHICS IN CHRISTIAN PERSPECTIVE

ROBERT C. ROBERTS

CASCADE *Books* • Eugene, Oregon

VIRTUE ETHICS IN CHRISTIAN PERSPECTIVE

Cascade Companions

Copyright © 2024 Robert C. Roberts. All rights reserved. Except for brief quotations in critical publications or reviews, no part of this book may be reproduced in any manner without prior written permission from the publisher. Write: Permissions, Wipf and Stock Publishers, 199 W. 8th Ave., Suite 3, Eugene, OR 97401.

Cascade Books
An Imprint of Wipf and Stock Publishers
199 W. 8th Ave., Suite 3
Eugene, OR 97401

www.wipfandstock.com

PAPERBACK ISBN: 978-1-4982-0798-0
HARDCOVER ISBN: 978-1-4982-0800-0
EBOOK ISBN: 978-1-4982-0799-7

Cataloguing-in-Publication data:

Names: Roberts, Robert Campbell, 1942– [author].

Title: Virtue ethics in Christian perspective / Robert C. Roberts.

Description: Eugene, OR: Cascade Books, 2024 | Series: Cascade Companions | Includes bibliographical references.

Identifiers: ISBN 978-1-4982-0798-0 (paperback) | ISBN 978-1-4982-0800-0 (hardcover) | ISBN 978-1-4982-0799-7 (ebook)

Subjects: LCSH: Virtues. | Christian ethics. | Character—Religious aspects—Christianity. | Morals. | Emotions—Religious aspects—Christianity. | Religion—Ethics.

Classification: BJ1250 R63 2024 (paperback) | BJ1250 (ebook)

VERSION NUMBER 10/24/24

Unless otherwise noted, Scripture quotations are from the New Revised Standard Version (NRSV), copyright @ 1989, Division of Christian Education of the National Council of the Churches of Christ in the United States in the United States of America. Used by permission. All rights reserved.

CONTENTS

Preface | vii
Abbreviation | ix

PART ONE: INTRODUCTION TO VIRTUE ETHICS

1 What Is Ethics? | 3
2 What Is a Virtue? | 21
3 Virtues and Moral Outlooks | 40
4 Virtues and the Law of God | 59
5 Virtues as the Foundation of Ethics | 78

PART TWO: SOME CHRISTIAN VIRTUES

6 Faith, Hope, and Love | 99
7 Grateful Generosity and Forgivingness | 109
8 Courage, Self-Control, and Patience | 123
9 Compassion, Gentleness, and Kindness | 135
10 Truthfulness, Justice, and Loyalty | 147
11 Joy, Wisdom, and Humility | 159

Postscript: Christian Virtue Ethics | 171

Afterword | 175
Bibliography | 177

PREFACE

I INTEND THIS BOOK as an accessible introduction to "virtue ethics." Virtue ethics is a philosophical discipline that centers on human virtues. Human virtues are developmental excellences that fit us to live a good and distinctively human life. They are a major key to our happiness and well-being.

Our well-being has several dimensions for which our character needs to fit us. We live in social groups. We depend on one another for information and cooperation. We care about what other people think and feel about us and how they act toward us. We need to respect others and to be respected by them. Resources are limited and need to be distributed among us in ways that are just. We give and receive gifts, and our well-being depends on our doing so well. We are troubled and vulnerable, and often need help. We make moral mistakes and need to forgive and be forgiven. Our lives contain risks and dangers that we must be able to navigate with confidence and grace. We have urges that are badly timed or not good for us or others and we must be able to control them. We live in time, and so need virtues like patience and perseverance.

The ancient Greek philosophers thought philosophy could help us become wise and good. Philosophy is thinking hard about things, and one of the most important things to think about is our own lives. What kind of beings are we, and what does it take for us to live well the life we find ourselves living? Are we doing it right? Are our lives promoting our good and the human good—or something else? How do we best become excellent and fulfilled human beings? Which qualities of character are virtues that make life good, and which ones are vices that damage us and our fellow creatures? How do the virtues make life good and the vices ruin it? This book follows the ancient Greeks in deploying philosophy—thinking hard about these questions—to promote living well.

In naming and sketching the qualities that are deep human excellences, this book is guided by the New Testament. It is a discussion of Christian virtue ethics. It accepts the ancient Greek philosophers' idea that thinking hard about the virtues can help us become virtuous. This agenda in philosophical ethics is rather different from mainline philosophical ethics and from contemporary virtue ethics, both of which tend to be attempts to find a conceptual grounding for ethical thought and life. In chapter 5, as a way of putting this book and its argument further in perspective, I explain the conceptual grounding project and contemporary virtue ethics as an example of it.[1]

---

1. I am grateful to Robin Parry for his insightful and well-informed editing of this book and to Aaron Hill for help with a point in chapter 7.

ABBREVIATION

NE   Aristotle, *Nicomachean Ethics*. Translated with an introduction by David Ross, revised by J. L. Ackrill and J. O. Urmson. Oxford: Oxford University Press, 1998

PART ONE
INTRODUCTION TO VIRTUE ETHICS

Chapter 1

WHAT IS ETHICS?

LIVING THINGS HAVE NEEDS

The earth teems with living things. And they come in so many kinds! Plants and animals, insects and fungi, microbes, and many diverse kinds of each of these broader kinds: trees and grasses, bears and mice and reptiles and birds, beetles and ants, bacteria and viruses, mushrooms and molds . . . But all living things have one thing in common: each kind, and each kind-within-a-kind, requires its own specific conditions to live well. They need their special kind of habitat, a certain limited temperature range, their specific foods and water, and the company of other plants and animals, of their own species and of other species.

Living things have these needs, which are specific to their species, because they are constantly changing. They use up food and process water, and most of them use light. All develop across time. They grow up. They have a lifespan. They start out as a seed or an embryo or an egg or whatever, and then develop in the direction of maturity. Eventually, they die. As they go through their age stages, their roles in their communities change. The goodness of their lives depends on their changing well, and ultimately on their dying well. If a seed doesn't have the right conditions, it won't grow into a tree, or it may grow into a stunted or sick tree, or a tree that doesn't reproduce. And the same seems to be true of all the plants and animals.

The "higher" animals also have *psychological* needs: they will live well only if they've been properly nurtured by their parents and other community members, only if they've had certain kinds of interactions with these others, and only if they continue to have such interactions. A dog that has had traumatic experiences of neglect and violence in its puppyhood will fall short of living up to its potential (i.e., a life that's a good life for a dog). By such interactions, individual higher animals acquire qualities that foster and betoken their living well. For example, the dog becomes trusting and confident and, if female, becomes capable of nurturing her own puppies.

In a comparable but much profounder way, we human beings need to grow up among people who love and respect others, who are patient and kind and courageous, and we need to become people with these same qualities. Only if we acquire these and other good personal traits will we have a life that is really good for us and our fellow human beings. We need friends and family who love and respect and understand us and we need to be friends and family to others, and we need to understand them. We need to be able to trust others and to be trustworthy. We need to be treated fairly and we need to want to treat others fairly and know how to do it. We need to be told the truth with regularity, because we rely on one another for information, and we need to be truthful with others who rely on us. When we are suffering or weak, we need to be helped, and we need to help others when they are suffering or weak. We need to be corrected by people who understand more than we do, and to be forgiven for our mistakes and transgressions so that we may be restored in the relationships that are so important to our living well as members of our species. And we need to forgive others their transgressions against us, so that we can continue to live in harmony with them. We need to live among models of such human excellences as these, and we need to be models of these excellences for others. We might become wealthy and powerful and even famous without these qualities, but that's not the same as having a good life.

The psychological needs that I've mentioned are all needs for "community." We need healthy two-way relationships with others. We need to belong to others and be with others who belong to us. And for this two-way belonging to meet our needs and the needs of the others who belong to us and to whom we belong, we need to love and respect and honor one another. We need mutuality, reciprocity, and communion with other human beings.

ETHICS

What, then, is ethics? Let's distinguish three answers to this question. In one sense, ethics is *the patterns of interaction among persons that constitute living well as a human community*. People who are living an ethical life are contributing in a healthy way to the lives of those around them and responding properly to the contributions that others make to their lives. In this way, we are living a life that's good for others and for that very reason good for ourselves. We tell each other the truth and respect each other's property and other rights. We help others in need and graciously receive others' help. We give generously to others. We pay our bills and work hard. We forgive others who wrong us. In the way we live, we contribute to and enjoy human well-being. Ethics, then, is living well in our community and more broadly in the human community. The Greek word for ethics means "custom"—a patterned way of living—and the philosophy of ethics is a study of customs that make for living well.

Ethics can also be thought of as *what guides persons to live ethically*. In turn, we can think of this guidance in two ways. One way is to think of it as *a set of rules for living well*—the moral law, so to speak. The Bible depicts Moses as receiving the law from God. In Exod 20 and Deut 5 we find a summary of that law: ten commandments. You shall do this, you shall refrain from that, and if you follow these rules, you'll have a good life. The philosopher Immanuel Kant (1724–1804) and many other modern philosophers have thought of ethics as the rules or principles for living well. Many species of living things have patterns of interaction among their members that constitute their living well. Only human beings have and need ethics in the sense of explicit rules to govern our actions by.

Every organism has its way of conducting its life, the patterns of behavior and response that are characteristic for the species, and that way is ordained by the animal's nature. By nature, beavers build dams and lodges, mosquitoes suck blood from other animals, trees root in the ground, photosynthesize, and produce their special kinds of seeds and fruits. Earthworms do their thing, buffalo theirs, frogs theirs, and so forth for all the species—except the humans. Most creatures' activity of living out its life tracks its nature more or less automatically. This is why most animals don't need ethics. They don't need to formulate rules to guide them to the good life. Their patterns of life are not an ethics because they have no alternative. Their life and their nature go hand in hand. They don't need to inquire about what kind of life they should live, because it just happens. But we human beings enjoy no such automatic attunement with our nature. We easily go off the tracks with actions that make us miserable and damage our relationships with one another, weaken our well-being, and even destroy us. This is why we need ethics: we need guidance. Ethics in this sense keeps us on track with our human nature.

In chapter 4, I'll argue that a deeper purpose of the law is not ultimately to provide formulas that we can consult when we want to know what to do. Instead, it trains our minds and hearts in ways of thinking, desiring, feeling, and paying attention. When this training is successful, it makes us wise about the situations of life. The prophet Jeremiah (31:33) says that in a new covenant God intends to write the law on the hearts of his people so that they spontaneously think and do and feel what makes for a good life for everybody. The people won't have to consult a rule book that says, "Do this" and "Don't do that." They'll be guided by the well-ruled tendencies of their hearts: their virtues of justice, compassion, generosity, forgiveness, truthfulness, and so forth. And they'll have these dispositions because *God* has "written" them on their hearts. These personal ways of being ready for life arise from interactions with God: in particular, acts of worship and blessing. In the Sermon on the Mount (Matt 5–7), Jesus seems to say that the real purpose of the law is not just to secure behavioral conformity, but to form inward attitudes and inclinations. Don't merely avoid killing people—don't even feel vengeful towards them. Don't fantasize about getting revenge. Don't take pleasure in the misfortune of your "enemy." Don't just refrain from having sex with people other than your spouse—be faithful to your spouse in your heart.

So, we can think of ethics as (1) patterns of interaction in good human life, and (2) what guides those interactions, which may be (a) rules or (b) inward dispositions. But we can also think of ethics in a third way: as what we're doing in this book. (3) Ethics is thinking hard and rigorously about (1) and (2). It's *a philosophical activity*, an investigation conducted by asking questions and trying out answers. The questions of ethics in this sense will be: What is the good life for human beings? And: What is it that guides persons in the conduct of this good life and allows them to implement such guidance?

Since this book is about Christian virtue ethics, we will be asking: What does Christianity say the good life is? What are the character traits that dispose and enable us to live a good life? How and to what extent are we responsible for living well, and what is God's role in our living well? Since our activity is philosophy, our conversation will also include people who are not Christians, but who have thought carefully about ethical questions.

AN ORDER OF PEACE

Christians and other theists (Jews, Muslims, Sikhs, and Hindus) believe that, in addition to our need for relationships with our fellow creatures, we have a psychological need for a relationship with God, our creator and savior and the governor of the universe—a relationship of love, respectful attention, obedience, gratitude, and trust.

Christians and Jews call the order of relationships or communion with God and fellow creatures that I have just described *shalom*, an order of peace and well-being. We also call it the *kingdom of God* or the *kingdom of heaven* or *eternal life* or the *new creation* or *blessedness*. The new creation is that order of relational life in which all is well.

Human creatures who live in this order are fully human in their flourishing because of their relationships to one another and because they are honoring and glorifying God with something approaching the honor and glory that is due him. When Jesus says, "Blessed are the peacemakers" and "Blessed are the pure in heart," he's talking about the kind of people who reflect, in their persons, and contribute to, such an order of peace. Terms like "kingdom of God" and "eternal life" and "new creation" imply that the relationship with God is central, and that it somehow qualifies and gives a special character to people's relationships with their fellow creatures in such an order of peace.

The healthy relationships I've mentioned are possible only to the extent that the parties to the relationships are fit enough to participate in them. You can't be a participating member of a soccer team unless you have the fitness to play soccer. If you don't, you won't last, you won't fit in, and you won't like it. You won't have the attitudes and abilities that befit soccer. The apostle Paul notes that people who are prone to "fornication, impurity, licentiousness, idolatry, sorcery, enmities, strife, jealousy, anger, quarrels, dissensions, factions, envy, drunkenness, carousing, and things like these . . . will not inherit the kingdom of God" (Gal 5:19-22 NRSV). *Of course* they won't. People with these tendencies are unfit to participate; they would disrupt the peace, and wouldn't even like it! They'd be like fish out of water, or like an overweight, out-of-shape, couch potato who is ignorant of the rules of soccer getting it into his head to take a position on a soccer team. His personal qualities make him unfit to participate.

What personal qualities does it take for a person to fit into the kingdom of God and pursue life there with eagerness and joy? In the next verses, Paul gives some examples of attitudes that fit a person to participate in an order of peace: love of one another, joy in what is truly good, patience, kindness, love of peace, generosity, trustfulness and trustworthiness, gentleness, and self-control (Gal 5:22–23). In other letters, Paul highlights still other qualities: compassion, forbearance, thankfulness, hopefulness, hospitality, forgivingness, wisdom, truthfulness, and humility. By contrast, opposite qualities would make life in an order of peace difficult if not impossible: cruelty, impatience, ingratitude, despair, xenophobia, racism, sexism, vengefulness, foolishness, being untruthful, and arrogance.

The traditional name of the good qualities that Paul commends is "virtues" and we call their opposites "vices." In chapter 2, we'll examine what these diverse qualities are "made of"—what kind of psychological qualities virtues and vices are.

PAGAN VIRTUE

Although the Bible, including the Old Testament (see especially the book of Proverbs), is full of references to qualities that enable us to participate well in an order of peace, philosophers tend to go back to ancient Greece for the origins of thinking about human virtues and vices. Socrates, Plato, and Aristotle are the main sources.

Socrates, who didn't write anything we know of, spent the latter years of his life having conversations with fellow citizens. He tried to get them to think about their lives: What kind of life is worthy to be lived by a human being? Are you living a life worthy of a human being? Many of his fellow citizens were living as though the most important things in life were money, reputation, and staying alive as long as possible. They were neglecting the development of their souls in such qualities as wisdom, justice, and courage. To be a real human being, thought Socrates, you need such qualities, whereas you can be wealthy and famous and live to a ripe old age while being a flop as a person. Surely, the Number One task of every human being is to become a *complete* human! Looking back on your life when it's coming to an end and thinking, "Well, at least I made a lot of money" or "Well, at least I was pretty famous," isn't very satisfying. And why not? Something in our nature seems to be seeking more. What is that "more"? The Bible calls it "glory." Socrates seems to have had a glimpse of glory. Glory is radiant excellence, excellence that smacks you with joyful admiration if you have eyes to see it or ears to hear it. The glory that I think Socrates must have caught sight of was the radiant excellence of a mature human being (Plato, *Phaedrus* 244a–256e).

Plato, in contrast with his teacher Socrates, wrote quite a bit and did so beautifully. Most of his writings are dialogues: conversations. They are about subjects like whether virtue can be taught and whether virtue is one single trait or many, the nature of particular virtues such as justice, courage, wisdom, temperance, friendship, and love, and related topics like the nature of knowledge. In other words, these dialogues are about excellence in being human. Many of them, especially the ones Plato wrote early in his career, feature Socrates as the main character. They are the principal source of our knowledge about Socrates, who seems to have been mainly interested in rigorous thinking about life as a way of self-cultivation. Plato's thought, especially as he got older, was more about very broad and deep questions like the ones we think of as typically philosophical—for example: What is the fundamental nature of things? Can anything be known? and What are the foundations of ethics?

Aristotle was a student of Plato. He was one of the most amazing thinkers in human history. He wrote about most of the topics of philosophy and science: the fundamental nature of reality (metaphysics), physics, psychology, biology, astronomy, politics, literary criticism, and public speaking (rhetoric). In all these areas he was influential, not just in his own time but down through the ages. But today his most widely read writing is his work about ethics, especially his *Nicomachean Ethics*, which I'll cite frequently in these pages.

Aristotle focuses on the question, what is the good life for human beings? His word for the good life is *eudaimonia* (you-dīmon-ía). The word is a composite of *eu*, which means excellent, and *daimōn*, a god or goddess. Eudaimonia means something like "having divine favor," "blessedness," "prosperity," "being lucky," "happiness," or "the good life." Aristotle thought that all of us, naturally and without prompting, want and seek eudaimonia. He agrees with Socrates in thinking that many people have wrong ideas about the good life. One of the aims of philosophy is to figure out the right idea so that we can pursue happiness with more definite purpose and a more effective approach. Aristotle's main point is that the way to achieve happiness is to become a person of virtue. You will experience eudaimonia and contribute to the eudaimonia of your community only if you become a wise, just, liberal (that is, generous), courageous, and temperate person.

We saw that the biblical idea of the good life is an order of peace (*shalom*) in which people relate to one another in ways that are good for everybody. Aristotle's notion of eudaimonia is similar. Eudaimonia is a social and interactive way of being that is good for all the citizens of a *polis* or city-state. It requires a certain character development in the individual. In chapter 3 we'll look at some ways that eudaimonia differs from shalom and that the Christian virtues differ from the Aristotelian virtues.

But our present question is about what ethics is, and especially about philosophical inquiry into ethics. Socrates went about asking people pointed questions about how to live, and in the course of that questioning he called *their* lives into question, so that they had to ask themselves whether they were living the best life. His work was a combination of objective inquiry and personal challenge. He was both investigating the good life and acting as a sort of therapist or pastor who helps people achieve it. He called himself a midwife—one who helps others give "birth" to their own wisdom, just as a literal midwife helps a woman give birth to her child. Plato's early dialogues are records or examples of Socrates' philosophical inquiry and they bring out the challenging or therapeutic aspect of Socrates' interactions with people. Aristotle's *Nicomachean Ethics* is more in the style of scientific or objective philosophical inquiry, but even he comments that the ultimate point of his inquiry is not just that we find out something about ethics, but that we become good (*NE* 2.2).

We are inquiring about the good life and what it takes to have one. That doesn't seem to be what the biblical writers are up to. They aren't trying to *figure out* what the good life is, but are struggling to *live* it and to help their fellow human beings live it—to be "saved" and to help God save others. The prophets and the apostles are not philosophers, but something closer to pastors. They may, no doubt, inquire about this or that along the way, but their main role is to direct and live their lives well and help the persons under their charge live well.

By contrast, in this book we are engaged in philosophical inquiry. We're interested in refining our understanding of the biblical view of moral character, and in comparing it with other outlooks and learning from them. But at the same time, we may hope that our thinking and questioning, like that of Socrates, will lead to improvement in our wisdom and other virtues.

VOCATIONS

People sometimes work for money. This is understandable, because we need food, after all, and shelter from cold and storms, and other things, and money is a common way to get them. But when we work *just* for money, we don't call the work our vocation. For many people, delivering pizzas while in college isn't a vocation; it's just a way to make money.

Other lines of work are more likely to be called vocations or callings. Teaching, for example, is naturally called a vocation. Carpentry, music, journalism, social work, psychology, the practice of law, medicine, engineering, computer programming, truck-driving, and many other useful activities are called vocations. In the Roman Catholic Church, to say that you have a vocation can mean that you're training for the priesthood. You have been called to it.

Having a vocation to a certain line of activity seems to presuppose two things: First, that it's a good fit for you. You have the talent. You can be trained. Second, there's some significant life-point to the activity. If you have a vocation, it will be to an activity that makes a contribution—to eudaimonia, to an order of peace.

One of the indications that you have a vocation is some special talent that sets you apart a little bit from other people. If you're good with numbers, that might be a sign that you're called to be an accountant or a math teacher. If you're especially good with your hands, perhaps you should take up carpentry or some other line of work that is served by fine motor skills.

You can see the word "voice" in the word "vocation." A vocation is a *calling*: literally, *somebody* is calling on you to follow a certain line of activity. "As Jesus passed on from [Nazareth], he saw a man called Matthew sitting at the tax office; and he said to him 'follow me.' And he rose and followed him" (Matt 8:9). Jesus calls and Matthew responds. Matthew has a vocation—and it's not tax collecting! It's easy to see how vocation can be associated with priesthood. But Protestants, especially under the influence of the reformer John Calvin, have tended to think that God calls people to many different lines of work: carpentry, music, and so forth—maybe even to tax collecting! And this is because any honest line of work can contribute to the kingdom of God.

The virtue-ethical point, however, is not just that your work contributes to the kingdom of God, but that you have a *sense* of that calling: you connect it, in your own thinking, with the purposes of God. That sense or feeling or knowledge of being called to your work constitutes a personal relationship to God and to those whom you serve in your work. It is your obedience to the call and the caller. It is an understanding that connects your work to God as the one who has called you, and to the people your work serves. Your sense of calling is a kind of wisdom. It affects how you do the work. It gives a special quality to the joy and satisfaction you take in your work.

Even delivering pizzas might be a vocation if you understand it as service to others and to God. It becomes a reverence to God and service to your fellow human beings. In that case, pizza deliveries aren't just a task to get done efficiently, while also getting as big a tip as possible, but also a service to fellow human beings, an expression of your love, your generosity, your compassion toward them. Pizza isn't the only thing they're hungry for. Your respect and love can nourish them as well. You want those pizzas to be delivered with gracious smiles and words of well-wishing: the customers aren't just potential tippers, but hungry people like you, whose hearts may be gladdened by an encouraging word with their hot pizza.

Think of how odd it would be if somebody asked what you're called in life to do, and you answered, "Make money." How could you be called to make money?! Well, you might be called to make money to finance vaccines for third world countries, to make possible an independent career in art or journalism or some other calling. But if the "point" of your work is just to make and accumulate wealth or fame for yourself, then it's not a vocation, not a calling. And the reason, according to Aristotle and Judaism and Christianity, is that it's not a contribution to eudaimonia or an order of peace. If your purpose is simply to become rich or famous, there's no way to pursue it generously, gratefully, compassionately, justly, and truthfully. These virtues all involve loving something other, and better, than money and fame.

This book is not about vocations, but about a single vocation, one that you, as well as everybody else, have whether you know it or not. You are called. Furthermore, it's your calling because of what you're like; but the quality that makes you fit for this calling isn't any special talent that sets you apart from other people, but a quality you share with everybody: being a human being.

Socrates, Plato, and Aristotle thought that we human beings are not completely human—not fully grown up, so to speak—until we are wise, just, brave, temperate, and pious. These five qualities later became known as the "cardinal virtues," the virtues on which our true humanity hinges (*cardō*, *cardinis*, hinge [Latin]). Christians later looked at the Greek list of virtues and thought, "OK, those are good qualities, but they don't capture everything about true human maturity." And, consulting the Christian Scriptures, they thought, a human isn't complete without faith in God, hope for the order of God's peace, and love of God and his creation, especially our fellow human creatures.

The notion of a *call* to maturity, of being called to be virtuous and contribute to an order of peace, is less clear in the ancient Greek philosophers than it is in the Bible. (Though it's pretty clear in Socrates, as he testifies in his speech to the jury that condemns him to death. See Plato, *Apology*.) But it's crystal clear from the Hebrew Scriptures that God called Israel to a life of righteousness and holiness as regulated by the Mosaic law, and it's clear in the New Testament that, in proclaiming the arrival of the kingdom of heaven in his own person, Jesus called anyone who has ears to hear to become a participant in and contributor to that glorious order of peace. And in calling us, he calls us also to become fit for such participation—to become generous, compassionate, forgiving, truthful, just persons.

CUSTOMS

Our word "ethics" comes from a Greek word for custom (*ēthos*). A custom is a habitual or patterned way of doing things. When you become accustomed to doing things in a customary way, the custom has become a personal habit, a tendency of your mind, your heart, even your body. The idea of regularity or pattern is built into the idea of a custom. A custom must be somewhat entrenched in a culture or a person or a family. Otherwise, it may be a way of doing things, but it isn't a custom.

Some customs are pretty trivial. In many places, including America, it's customary to place the knife and the spoon on the right side of the plate and the fork on the left. It wouldn't matter much if we did it some other way. Other customs are indispensable. In fact, some are so important that we insist on people following them, even though not everybody does. We look down on and even punish people who flout such customs as paying one's bills and taking care of one's own children. People who defy these customs get in trouble. We try not to let them get away with it. We have laws requiring people to honor such customs.

You might think, these are not just customs. They're obligations! Ethics is about obligations, not customs.

You have a point. To say that a pattern of behavior or thinking is a custom is, in English, to suggest that it's *not* obligatory. Yet, I think we retain much of the Greek idea of *ēthos* in our "ethics." We think that ethical patterns of behavior and thought will be effective only if they are entrenched in our patterns of social interaction—our dealings with our neighbors, with our children, with our colleagues and business associates. To be effective, the patterns need to have become "customs" among us. And this can be so only if we individuals have become so accustomed to dealing with one another according to ethical patterns that our thinking, our feeling, and our acting have been infused with these ethical patterns. Ethical customs need to have become resident in our minds and hearts. They need to have become our spontaneous and natural ways of thinking, feeling, and acting.

An ethical life is a pattern of thinking, feeling, and acting that makes for a life that's good for everybody—both the person who's doing the thinking, feeling, and acting and the people he or she thinks and feels about, and whose lives are touched by his or her actions and emotions. And ethics, as philosophical questioning about ethical life, is research about *which* patterns of thought, feeling, and action contribute to a happy and prosperous life, and which ones go against such a life. That's why ethics is about customs. That's why ethics needs to be not just about what we should *do* but also about what kind of persons we should *be*. That's why ethics is about the virtues.

CONCLUSION

Ethics, as we'll pursue it in this book, is the study of the kind of living that befits a human being. It's an effort to answer a question, which can be phrased in different ways:

- What is it, most fundamentally, to be a success in life?
- What is it to be a fully formed human being, a grown-up?
- What is to be a contributing member of a healthy community, to live well, to be happy?

To answer this question, we must investigate the personal qualities that fit a person for such participation. We must try to understand both what those qualities are and why a person with those qualities is happy and tends to promote well-being in people whose lives intersect with hers. Traditionally, those qualities have been called virtues. In chapter 2, we'll address the question what kind of quality a virtue is.

FOR DISCUSSION

1. How is ethics like and unlike the "demands" that have to be satisfied for animals and plants of various species to flourish?
2. What are the three senses of "ethics," according to Roberts, and how are they related to one another?

PART ONE: INTRODUCTION TO VIRTUE ETHICS

3. Name and discuss some ways that Christian ethics is like and unlike pagan ethics as represented by the ancient Greek philosophers.

4. How is ethics "customary" and a matter of "vocation"?

Chapter 2

WHAT IS A VIRTUE?

EQUIPPED FOR LIVING A HUMAN LIFE

Let's begin with some thoughts inspired by Aristotle. A virtue, in the broadest sense, is a good quality or feature of something. "Good for what?" you ask. Good for whatever the something is for. When we manufacture things, we have some purpose in mind, and we try to give them qualities that serve that purpose. Those qualities are virtues. For example, knives are typically made for cutting. A good knife has qualities that serve that purpose: a comfortable handle and a blade that can be sharpened and retains its sharpness through a period of use. The comfort of the handle and the sharpenability of the blade are virtues in a knife because of what a knife is for. If a knife has those qualities, then to that extent it's a good one.

Living things such as plants and animals can be good or less good specimens. For example, it's good for a rat to have four legs. You say, "Rats are vermin, and I wish there weren't any." Well, maybe for your purposes that's so; but what about the rats? When it comes to living things, *our* purposes for them don't count. The purposes that set the standards for their excellence are *their* purposes. For example, one of the purposes of a rat (from its own perspective, so to speak) is to protect itself from predators. For that purpose, its having four legs is an excellence. A rat that's born with only three good legs will be less excellent at escaping predators. Other purposes built into rat nature are gathering food and reproducing their species. Qualities that make them fit for these functions will be rat excellences (rat virtues). So a good rat will have a sharp sense of smell and good teeth and well-functioning reproductive organs.

Because the natural purposes of rats, like most other living things, are so immediately tied to their survival, almost all rats have the rat virtues. Rats that lack the rat virtues are pretty quickly eliminated, so most of the members of the population are about equally virtuous.

Not so among human beings. As the Bible notes, we don't live by bread alone (Deut 8:3). The purpose of human life isn't survival of the species, but glorifying God and so being glorified ourselves. We'll say more about glory in a moment. We "live" by words, by thoughts, by concerns that *we* endorse, by actions that *we* perform. We live by accepting traditions that our elders pass on to us. We live by knowledge of ourselves, knowledge that we can leverage in the interest of becoming something better than we currently are. We live by our philosophies of life, our worldviews. We live by our sensitivity to our fellow human beings and our attitudes of respect or contempt, of fear of them or hope for them, and much more. In all these things, we live by words that come to us from God, and from our praise of God. All this gives scope for great variability in virtue among human beings. A few people are very virtuous, and a few very evil, and most of us fall somewhere on a continuum between these extremes.

Four-leggedness in a rat is achieved totally without the rat's intervention or choice. But faith, hope, kindness, generosity, courage, justice, humility, and many other human virtues are achievements resulting from our repeated choices, efforts, and reflection. At the same time, if we are fortunate, we are helped in the formation of these virtues by the respect, love, training, and teaching that we receive from others who have become good and responsible people by *their* repeated choices, efforts, and reflection. For these reasons, the variability of virtue among human beings is great.

Virtues are completions. The rat with only three legs is an incomplete rat, and the person who lacks humility or courage or justice is an incomplete human being. She isn't living a fully human life. Consider another biological comparison. A fertile acorn is in a sense already an oak. The sense is this: it's a *potential* oak tree. To be an actual and complete oak tree, the acorn needs to acquire some qualities—bark, a trunk, branches, leaves, and eventually little flowers and acorns. To acquire these qualities, it needs time and some conditions: decent soil, water, light, and warmth. And as it grows, it does things: it takes in moisture and nutrients from the soil and the air, it puts out little buds that become leaves, and other buds that become flowers and then acorns. These processes are its living, its completion, and this living is what the original acorn was for. When it functions well in these ways, it's complete as an oak tree, and the dispositions to do these things well are its virtues.

This chapter isn't about rats or oak trees, but about us and the qualities we have when we are complete, mature, grown up, and functioning like real human beings.

PART ONE: INTRODUCTION TO VIRTUE ETHICS

VICES

Let's start on a negative note. I had a peach tree. In some ways, it seemed to be flourishing. A couple of years ago it was full of fruit. In fact, the growing peaches were weighing it down so much that I was afraid it would break. One night, when the peaches were about three-quarters grown, a windstorm came through and the tree did break. But it wasn't just a branch here and there, as I had feared. It broke off *at the trunk*! It was a total disaster. When I looked at the broken trunk, the center—the heartwood, which provides the primary strength of the tree—was rotten. It was literally "rotten to the core." The tree wasn't very old. It should have been in the prime of its life, as it appeared to be. But in fact that tree, full of fruit, was as good as dead. It was a pushover.

People, too, can be rotten at the core. In fact, Jesus teaches that *only* at the core can we be truly rotten—rotten *as people*. The word "vice" can sound old-fashioned. People used to use it for bad habits like smoking and gambling. But real vices are a lot worse than that. They are growths of death in the heart of a person, like the rotten heartwood of my tree. Smoking is bad for you, but it doesn't undermine your personhood. (Come to think of it, though, gambling probably does.)

Some Pharisees and scribes noticed that Jesus's disciples were eating without washing their hands in the manner prescribed by a rabbinic Jewish tradition. Jesus took the occasion to criticize people who violate the law of God by replacing it with one of these human traditions. For example, one tradition says you can withhold support from your ageing parents if you say the money is dedicated to God. In other words, you don't have to honor your father and mother, as God requires in the fifth commandment (Exod 20:12). Similarly, the tradition requires you to wash your hands to purify yourself. Insisting on this tradition distorts our thinking about personal purity and pollution. What is the proper way to think about it?

Jesus said, "It's what comes *out* of a person that pollutes the person. For out of the heart of a person come evil desiring thoughts: adulteries, fornications, murders, thefts, covetousness, wickedness, treachery, indecency, the evil eye, blasphemy, arrogance, foolishness. All these bad things emerge from the *inside* of a person and pollute him" (Mark 7:20–23, my translation). And so, Jesus argued, the food that goes into the stomach doesn't corrupt the person essentially. It's the thoughts and desires that originate in the heart of a person and are expressed in bad actions that make for essential personal defilement.

Vices are heart conditions, defects in the functioning of the heart of a human being. They are person weaknesses, just as rotten heartwood is the fundamental tree weakness. Smoking and eating with dirty hands aren't vices in this sense. Vices are disastrous for a human life, even though, like my peach tree, the person may give the outward impression of being hale and hearty. What makes vices so disastrous? They attack the very heart of a person because that human heart is created to be ordered by the thoughts and desires that mark shalom, the order of peace, the love of God and all that God loves. The desiring thoughts that constitute the vices are all opposed, in one way or another, to the ones that mark the order of peace. They corrupt the heart because they turn the heart towards disordering distortions of the true good.

The main virtues, too, are heart conditions, in this case, healthy ones. Like the heartwood of a tree when it's sound, the human virtues—humility, gentleness, justice, truthfulness, forgivingness, forbearance—are the core strengths of a human person. They are dispositions to think clearly about the good in the situations of life, and to care deeply about that good. I call the main virtues "core" for two reasons: (1) they are central in that the other dispositions derive from them or are in their service; and (2) they form the living core of the mature and real human being.

VIRTUES AND VICES ARE NOT ACTIONS, BUT DISPOSITIONS

What is a disposition? In a book titled *The Concept of Mind*, the philosopher Gilbert Ryle illustrates the idea of a disposition with the tendency of glass to shatter. Unless it's specially treated to make it shatterproof, glass is *brittle*. Brittleness is the disposition of glass to shatter under some conditions: for example, the glass has to be cool enough, and it has to be hit by something hard enough with sufficient force. Brittleness is a readiness or tendency or disposition of glass to shatter when such conditions prevail. It's an if-then quality: *glass is brittle* equals *if* the conditions prevail, *then* glass shatters. The brittleness is not an event (say, the event of shattering), but a readiness for a certain kind of event—shattering—to occur.

In a similar way, a virtue isn't a good action (an event that somebody performs) or an ethical feeling (say, righteous anger or virtuous hopefulness) that comes over you at a certain time. It's a disposition or readiness or tendency to perform actions of justice or generosity or feel emotions of a certain type, like compassion or righteous anger or hope for justice, under conditions of a certain type. What *kind* of disposition is a virtue?

Obviously, virtues are not physical qualities like having a beautifully shaped nose or a nice figure or being tall and muscular. Anyway, physical qualities are not in themselves dispositions, but states of the body, though being muscular is a basis of the disposition that we call strength, and no doubt states of the brain are bases of moral dispositions. No, virtues are broadly psychological qualities, qualities of the soul or mind.

The mind can have several kinds of qualities, some of which are dispositions. We have beliefs, thoughts, knowledge, emotions, desires, concerns, skills, attitudes, and personality traits. But you can have all the beliefs and skills necessary for being generous without being generous. You can have personality traits like being gregarious or shy, cheerful, irrepressibly optimistic, or thoughtfully introspective, whether or not you have virtues or vices. So these traits can't *be* the virtues.

Virtues are traits of character, and more specifically, moral character. Examples are truthfulness, compassion, fairness, self-control, courage, humility, and a sense of duty. Why are human virtues moral qualities, while the virtues of a rat are conditions of survival like having four legs and potent testicles? The answer is that what's basic to being human, and thus basic to human well-being (eudaimonia), is the fitness to live in an order of peace. I'll propose that virtues come in three kinds: *concerns* for the true good, *abilities* to manage our minds, and an emotional *indifference* to self-importance, which is a destructive pseudo-good. And I'll note that having certain thoughts is required for the virtuous concerns and abilities.

THREE KINDS OF HUMAN VIRTUE

a. Concerns for the Good

The core qualities that Jews and Christians regard as virtues are a matter of caring about the good. They are loves of the true good. "Seek first the kingdom of God," says Jesus. "Where your treasure is, there will your heart be also." I have noted that vices are heart disease and virtues are healthy heart conditions. Jesus's parables are often about seeking and finding, about hidden treasures, about lost lambs and coins and sons that, after some seeking, get found. Clearly, a person who seeks something cares about it, wants it, is concerned about it. The core virtues, according to the New Testament, are dispositions of the heart. Your heart is your mind, especially the part of it that makes for desires, emotions, interests, concerns, and the thoughts that express and shape them.

If we ask, "Why does the compassionate person start to help when he sees someone in need?" the answer is "Because he cares." Caring about shalom is a disposition of his heart, and someone in trouble is a flaw in the order of peace. The sufferer's suffering needs to be corrected. Virtuous persons cherish and seek the true good for themselves and their community.

The fact that virtuous people seek the *true* good implies that you must be wise to have the virtues. You have to *think correctly* about the good. For example, if you foolishly think that the good is beer and wild parties and sex at every opportunity, or the true good is becoming as wealthy as you can or being the winner in every contest, or having lots of power over others, or being famous, then you don't have the virtues, because the "good" you seek isn't the *true* good. Because of your distorted thinking, you have distorted concerns, a wayward heart. Your personal core isn't healthy, but weak and riddled with disease.

So the core virtues are all variants of *love:* love of God and God's kingdom, and consequently love of people, as well as love, appropriately adjusted, of the rest of God's creation.

b. Abilities of Self-Mastery

Second, we have supplementary virtues, especially ones that enable us to compensate for defects and shortcomings and badly targeted aims in our dispositions of concern for the good. We tend to have bad habits and urges that can work against our virtues of caring: distorted appetites for food and sex, concerns for unworthy objects that yield *unworthy* joy, anger, hope, fear, impatience, relief, and disappointment. We have vices that need to be healed.

We strive to be compassionate, generous, and forgiving, but we find that we are sometimes indifferent, stingy, and grudging. We have bad habits that we need to overcome. If we are to act virtuously, we must dodge and redirect these counterforces in the interest of being more virtuous. To succeed in these efforts, we need *abilities* to do so. Examples of such abilities are self-control, patience, perseverance (steadfastness), and courage. All of them are kinds of self-control, but with maturity, these powers can become so ingrained that they seem to happen automatically. If all the core virtues are variants of intelligent love, all the supplementary virtues are variants of intelligent self-control.

c. Purity of Heart

A third kind of virtue is humility in its various forms. It is neither a concern nor an ability, but the absence of some concerns that are particularly contrary to the love of God's kingdom. The love of self-importance in its various manifestations spoils all the virtues of caring for eternal life. Humility, then, is the purity of heart that consists in being *indifferent to self-importance*. Humility derives from the core virtues because the stronger they are, the weaker is the concern for self-importance.

Let's now think a little more deeply about the core virtues, the ones that consist in wise concerns for the good.

SEEKING THE ORDER OF PEACE, PIECE BY PIECE

a. Virtue Entire

As I noted in chapter 1, Aristotle identifies an order of living that he calls *eudaimonia*. In his thinking, eudaimonia is *the* (overall) good for us human beings. It's the order of true human life. This Greek word is often translated "happiness," and I think that's a good translation if we're careful about the meanings of "happiness" in English. We need to distinguish happiness as momentary joy from the happiness of a life that is well lived. In the first sense, an alcoholic homeless person might be "happy" to find a full bottle of wine in a trash can, but it seems implausible to say that she's a happy *person* or that she has a happy *life*. Eudaimonia, as Aristotle understands it, is happiness only in this second sense. Eudaimonia is the happiness of a well-formed person living in a well-formed social setting, for whom things are going well.

The central question of his *Nicomachean Ethics* is "What is eudaimonia and how do we achieve it?" He addresses this question because he thinks many of us are vague or downright mistaken about what eudaimonia is, and so don't know what we're looking for. Some people think that happiness is being rich, or being idle, or being always on vacation, or having lots of pleasure or power. We'll be more likely to achieve our goal if we have a clear conception of what we're seeking. The short answer to Aristotle's question is that eudaimonia is that order of human living in which the participants have the dispositions, primarily towards one another, of justice, friendship, liberality (Aristotle's version of generosity), courage, and temperance. In other words, the best and happiest life for human beings—both as individuals and as a society—is the life of virtues. So the question "What is eudaimonia?" comes down to the question "What are the virtues like?" and "What is it like to practice them?" And the question "How do you get eudaimonia?" comes down to the question "How do you acquire the virtues?"

The wise person is one who knows what eudaimonia is and, knowing it, cares about it as it is worthy to be cared for. In lovingly understanding the true good for human beings, the person of practical wisdom (the *phronimos*, as Aristotle calls him) has virtue entire. In being virtuous in this way, he understands how all the specific virtues work, psychologically, and how they contribute to the life of eudaimonia.

If the true good is eudaimonia, as Aristotle thinks, then the central virtues will be concerns for eudaimonia and specific aspects of it—for justice, for the well-being of the city-state and fellow citizens, for laws that serve the eudaimonia of the people, and for public works that make life good for people. You can see how important peace and order are by looking at Aristotle's discussion of the proper constitution of the city-state in his book *Politics*.

Aristotle's question "What is eudaimonia and how do we achieve it?" has the form of the basic question of virtue ethics. I say "form" because the idea of the good that is to be explored can vary (see ch. 3). For Christians, the question won't be about eudaimonia in particular, but about *our* concept of the ultimate good: the kingdom of God, eternal life, the order of true shalom. So the basic question of Christian virtue ethics will be "What is eternal life and how do we achieve it?"

If the good is the kingdom of God, as in the biblical vision, then the central virtues will be concerns for that kingdom and aspects of it: for the honor and worship of God, for the health and well-being of God's people (ultimately, all people), for the truth of God's kingdom to be known by all people, for material goods to be rightly shared, and for the relations among people to be harmonious, for example. Virtuous people will seek to understand well these aspects of the kingdom so that we can seek them more effectively: we will seek to be wise. We will be lovers of wisdom (in Greek, *philo-sophoi*), and thus lovers of virtues. We will care about knowledge of the good because that knowledge enables us to practice the good.

In chapter 3 we will explore more deeply the idea of correct thinking about the true good. We will compare the Christian way of thinking about the world, the self, and others—Christian wisdom—with some alternative views.

The biblical tradition has two names for the character of a person who is overall fit to live in and contribute to this order of truly human life. It calls this quality *righteousness* or *holiness*. The Greek word that is usually rendered "righteousness" in English translations of the Bible is the same as Aristotle's word for justice: *dikaiosynē*, which means something like "honoring what is right." The righteous person is one whose whole life and thinking is oriented by his intelligent seeking of shalom. Righteous people's love or concern for shalom, guided by their correct understanding of it, is what makes them fit to live in the order of shalom. The word "holiness" is similar to biblical "righteousness" except that it explicitly suggests separateness from what is not righteous, and association with what is most holy, namely, God.

Virtue entire, then, is seeking first God's kingdom: giving it priority in all your cares and decisions. This is the central aspiration of the person who represents the biblical ideal. Jesus of Nazareth is this person—the righteous man, the holy man, the man of practical Jewish wisdom. Above all and in everything that he seeks, he seeks the kingdom of God, the will of his Father, eternal life.

b. Virtues

The English word "disposition" contains the word "position," suggesting that *varying* dispositions or attitudes might be taken toward the *same* loved thing, depending on your position with respect to it, or its position with respect to you—your angle on it, so to speak. Your disposition toward someone you love can depend on whether the person

- Is hostile to you (love of enemies)
- Is an outsider in need of welcome (hospitality)
- Has offended you (forgiveness)
- Is an irritating person (forbearance)
- Is in trouble (compassion)
- Is vulnerable to something you might say or do (gentleness)
- Has done you some favor (gratitude)
- Is someone to whom something is owed (justice)
- Needs information or advice from you (truthfulness)
- Is just a person with whom you can share something good (generosity)

These are all dispositions that the loving person takes toward fellow human beings, depending on those peoples' differing positions relative to the loving person.

And so, the virtue of righteousness or holiness, which is a disposition towards eternal life or the kingdom of God, divides into more specialized dispositions—dispositions toward God as creator, provider, and loving Father (faith, hope, and love) and dispositions that address more specific appeals of our fellow human beings in their needs and vulnerabilities, in their situations and attitudes toward us. In taking any one of these specialized attitudes, and in acting on it, a person plays the role of a participant in eternal life, in the kingdom of God.

Let's look at compassion as an example of a specialized angle on loving God and your neighbor.

c. Example: Compassion

One day (Luke 10:25–37), a Jewish legal expert tested Jesus by asking, "How shall I inherit eternal life?" Jesus answered, "Well, what does the law say?" The expert replied, "Love the Lord your God with all your heart and your neighbor as yourself." Jesus said, "That's it: do that, and you'll live." But the expert, realizing that he'd been put on the defensive, tried to justify himself by asking, "Who is my neighbor?" It turns out that living—*really* living, in the sense of living *eternal* life—has a lot to do with being neighbors. So Jesus tells a story about a man with the heart of a neighbor.

A man was robbed and beaten half dead and left by the side of the road. Two people came walking along who had some training in the law of God, a priest and a Levite. They had studied God's outline for an order of peace. They could talk about it pretty accurately and understood it well enough. They knew what a neighbor was. They took a look at the bloody naked man moaning in the ditch, swerved around on the other side, and kept going. Then a foreigner came along, a Samaritan, and when he saw the injured man it wrenched his gut and he right away went to him and washed his bloody wounds with a little wine and soothed them with some oil. Then he took him to an inn and paid the innkeeper for a room where the man could rest, and promised to stop on his way back and pay any further expenses.

After telling this story, Jesus asked the expert, "Who was neighbor to the man in the ditch?" The expert had to admit that it was the compassionate Samaritan who loved God and his neighbor. In his response, the expert showed that he understood the commandment and the concept of a neighbor pretty well. By implication, he also understood the Jewish concept of eternal life, in his own way. Yet he seemed to be as much in the dark about eternal life as the priest and the Levite in Jesus's story. If he had been better attuned to eternal life, he wouldn't have been trying to trap Jesus.

THOUGHTS AND UNDERSTANDING

How could he be so full of understanding and so lacking in understanding at the same time? I think the answer lies in Jesus's teaching about the "heart." The Samaritan's heart was engaged in the kingdom of God, in this sense: in the kingdom of shalom, all is well, and the Samaritan saw, with the eyes of his heart (so to speak), that shalom needed to be restored to the man in the ditch. Because he cared that there be peace for all, he was moved by what he saw. The hearts of the priest and the Levite seemed to be engaged elsewhere. So we have two kinds of understanding. On the one side is the kind that the expert and the priest and the Levite had of eternal life. It's important, but it isn't enough for eternal life *itself*.

When Jesus says, "Do this, and you will *live*," he implies that you can understand in the expert's sense without *living* the eternal life, the life of the kingdom of God. In showing compassion and generosity toward the injured man, the Samaritan showed that he understood the kingdom of God in the very situations of his life. His caring about peace made him understand how important it was to help the man in the ditch. The kingdom of God is by its nature so lovable that if you don't love it, you don't understand it.

The person of practical wisdom, whether Aristotelian or Jewish, has a dual-focus understanding. On the one side, she keeps her eye on the big goal: eudaimonia or the order of peace. It regulates everything she thinks and does. But the situations of her life are all different from one another. Every day presents new challenges, and she must discern in the particular situations that confront her what eudaimonia or the order of peace would be. Because of her wisdom, she has good judgment about this: in many cases, she sees immediately what the kingdom requires. To the extent that she sees shalom reflected in her circumstances, she is satisfied and joyful, grateful, hopeful. To the extent that she sees in her circumstances the contrary of peace, she is distressed: sorry, regretful, guilty, sad, disappointed, angry, etc.

The Samaritan may have been less trained in the Jewish guidelines (ethical thoughts) than the expert, the priest, and the Levite, but with his heart he understood eternal life better than they did. I mentioned that the Samaritan showed compassion and generosity. These are personal qualities of someone who *cares about people* in the way that the Jewish guidelines prescribe. If the Samaritan is our model, compassion and generosity are ways of caring about people and God. As the legal expert in Jesus's conversation noted, it's all about *loving* God and people. To love is to care.

We feel emotions about what we care about. The emotion that the Samaritan feels in Jesus's story is the distress of compassion. This is not the same as the virtue of compassion. We can see this by extending Jesus's story in our imagination. Imagine that the Samaritan stops by the inn on his way back from his journey, to pay the innkeeper for the further expenses, and the innkeeper tells him that the injured man got better after a few days and left for a job that was waiting for him in a town down the road. Because of the Samaritan's same love of the order of peace that he earlier experienced in the discomfort of compassion, he now feels joy about the injured man's recovery and gratitude to the innkeeper for his good work and hope that the man will continue to prosper. The virtue of compassion manifests itself not only in the emotion of compassion, but also in joy, gratitude, hope, and many other types of emotion, depending on the ways particular situations affect the fortunes of an order of peace.

In the biblical understanding, the "heart" is where thoughts are hatched and brooded, but especially thoughts that are loaded with wishing, caring, desiring, and appreciating—thoughts about what is of interest and personal concern to us. The thoughts of the heart are good (virtuous) if the wish, care, or desire is for something good. The Samaritan's wish for the injured man to be well and at peace was expressed in his distress at seeing him lying in the ditch and his joy in hearing from the innkeeper about the man's recovery. The thoughts of the heart are evil if they are loaded with concerns that are contrary to the order of peace. For example, thoughts of revenge, cruel thoughts, contemptuous thoughts about fellow human beings. If you think with pleasure about ways to get revenge on your enemies, or if you take pleasure in thinking, "That person is a depraved fool" or "Those people are suckers and losers" or "That person is deranged and is a total failure," then your heart is evil and you need to repent and seek forgiveness. If, on the contrary, you rejoice with those who rejoice and weep with those who are in trouble, then the thoughts of your heart show you to be a loving person, a person of some virtue.

The main biblical virtues are rooted in caring about pieces (aspects) of the order of peace. We can call these virtues "substantive" because they are the moral substance of the good life, the life that belongs to a mature, complete, and well-formed human being. Here are some main biblical virtues:

- Righteousness (love of God and God's kingdom)
- Holiness (love of God and God's kingdom)
- Faith (trusting love of God and God's kingdom)
- Hope (confident expectation of God's kingdom)
- Compassion (hatred of others' suffering)
- Gentleness (care for others' vulnerability)
- Generosity (concern for others' pleasure and well-being)
- Gratitude (loving recognition of benefactors)
- Forgivingness (love of offenders)
- Enemy love (love of those who are hostile towards you)
- Honoring (celebration of others' humanity and excellence)
- Truthfulness (concern to know and communicate the truth)
- Justice (concern that people be given their due)

CONCLUSION

The main virtues are qualities of human maturity, qualities that allow us to function as real human beings. They are qualities that make us good at what we're for. According to

Jewish and Christian teaching, we are for living in an order of peace ruled by God. Where God rules our hearts, there is peace and harmony and love among human beings. The core or substantive virtues are dispositions to live that way. (See the list above.) A second group of virtues are abilities to manage our hearts so that they get on the track of the order of peace and stay there, despite various countermotives. Examples of these are self-control, patience, and perseverance. A third kind of virtue is humility, which is a purity or freedom of our hearts from the vices of pride.

The Christian virtues are structured by a particular way of thinking about human nature, the nature of the universe, and the nature of God. This framework is called biblical theology. This theology is not the only possible way of thinking about human maturity and the qualities that constitute it. In the next chapter we'll compare the biblical way of shaping a human mind with some alternative ways of doing so.

FOR DISCUSSION

1. What sort of thing is a virtue, according to Aristotle? What is a human virtue, and what is it for?

2. What is a vice, and what makes it bad?

3. Roberts speaks of three kinds of virtues. What are they? Can you think of any virtues that don't fit in one of the three kinds?

4. What does thinking have to do with the virtues?

5. How is the good Samaritan a lover of the order of peace? What are the signs of this in his emotional responses?

Chapter 3

VIRTUES AND MORAL OUTLOOKS

LOOKING OUT

Sometimes we're puzzled by the way people live. We say things like "I really don't know where he's coming from." "She lives in a different world." Such people strain our powers of empathy, our ability to understand them from the "inside."

Driving in the mountains, we sometimes come to a scenic outlook, a place where we can park the car, walk to a protected promontory, and survey, from on high, a vast area of landscape. Because we take in many things in a single view, we see them in their positions relative to one another. We see this village in the distance, and that one closer by. We see farmlands, forests and rivers, church steeples and town halls, all in a particular spatial arrangement. When we stand at the railing of a scenic outlook, it's a viewpoint, our standpoint, a perspective from which we see the countryside. We see what's out there and how its parts are disposed to one another, but we see it all from a particular angle. Two people standing on the same scenic outlook see the array below from the same perspective—the same things, disposed to one another in the same way.

Many miles down the road is another outlook from which we can see some of the same things, but other things as well. Now the church that was rather nearby in the valley below is off in the distance, barely visible, and the village that was in the far distance on the left is directly below us. We may even have to be told, or learn from a map, that it's the same village we saw earlier, so different does it look from this new perspective. We see different stretches of farmland and forest; or, if they are the same as we saw earlier, from this new perspective they look like different ones. We see villages that weren't visible from the other standpoint.

Moral outlooks are a little bit like scenic outlooks, except that the "perspective" isn't visual, but conceptual; the "seeing" is not with our eyes, but with our mind, and more particularly with our heart. The distances that we see between things in the visual outlook correspond to distances from the heart in the moral outlook: of something we love, we say, "It's close to my heart." It's in the foreground of my concerns or attachments. Of two friends we say, "They are very close." Sadly, we say, "She's not very close to her family." Of Jesus we say, "The poor were close to his heart." Some things matter more to us than others. They are more important, and our "heart" is the aspect of our mind in which this difference lives. It's the mental dimension that corresponds to spatial distance in the visual.

When we look out on the countryside from a scenic outlook, our minds organize what we see according to categories: there are rivers, towns, forests, prominent buildings, and so forth. From some scenic outlooks, some such categories will be unrepresented. No towns may be visible, or no rivers. In a similar way, a moral outlook is a standpoint from which we "see" various elements in our lives: our families, our friends, our work, our money and other possessions, our God, our neighbors (strangers and people we don't know well, people in need, people who dress differently than we do, or differ in skin color or mode of speech, and people who have something against us), physical and other pleasures, beauty, our work, our power, and perhaps other categories of things. From one moral outlook, some things may be invisible or nearly so, which from another moral outlook are prominent.

Once we get to a certain age, we human beings develop a moral perspective on life. It may be implicit: we might have a hard time articulating it or summing it up in a short paragraph. It's an intuitive mental map of the activity of living, a sense of what's most important, what's somewhat important, and what's not very important, and how the things in these shades relate one another. An outlook isn't a theory. Because of its being about life, and therefore about what matters and evokes concern and emotions, it's a *spirit*, a *breathing*, of the values of the "things" of living. Breathing is a constant accompaniment and source of life. If we breathe the Spirit of God, we derive God's life, taking it into our own. But it's possible, as well, to breathe a spirit of death, as we'll see in an example.

When you stand on the scenic outlook surveying the villages, the forests, the farms and rivers, it's part of your understanding of the scene that you see it as you do because of where *you* are standing. In the same way, the Christian who sees the neighbor, creation, and God in the perspective provided by the Christian moral outlook realizes that she sees the "world" as she does because of where she "stands"—because of her faith and its theology. The moral outlook provides for an understanding of our life, our soul (Mark 8:37). Or if, by empathy, we manage to "see" life from an outlook that's not our own, what we "see" is a possible life, or somebody else's soul. But even when the life on which you look out is your own soul, it's not all about you. Your life is populated with God and God's plan and will for the world, with your family, your friends, your colleagues, your enemies, and your neighbors, including the strange ones.

Our moral outlook may be very different from the outlooks of other people we know. That can help to explain why other people's ways of living can be so puzzling to us.

HEART AND MIND

In the first eleven chapters of Paul's letter to the Christians in Rome, Paul gives the richest account in all his letters of the gospel of Jesus Christ: God has revealed himself in a new way, embodying God's law in the perfectly obedient life of Jesus, thus casting light on our deep disobedience and so our shortfall from living the truly human life that is sketched in that law. God offers us the life that is in Jesus by a kind of friendship and proxy: we can share in the real living of Jesus by participating in him, by trusting him, by his lovingly dwelling in us, by our becoming slaves of his righteousness and so finding true freedom. We exist in the Spirit by setting our minds on the things of the Spirit, whether we are Jews or gentiles, and so we acquire the mind of Christ (1 Cor 2:16). Then in chapter 12, Paul begins a section on what all this means for Christians' daily living. He begins,

> Therefore, brothers and sisters, I appeal to you
> by God's compassion to present yourselves as

> a living offering, holy and acceptable to God, which is your reasonable [*logikos*] service. Don't be conformed to this age, but be transformed by the renewing of your minds, so that you may discern what is the will of God—what is good and acceptable and perfect. (Rom 12:1–2, my translation)

In this magnificent summary introduction, Paul invites Christian readers to follow up on the happy announcement of the first eleven chapters. In his "therefore," Paul scoops together all that he has said in the first eleven chapters and invites us into its personal consequence. He bids us to respond to God's loving compassion: what God has done and will do through Jesus. How does he propose that we do this?—By *giving* ourselves. We are to respond to God's generous giving of himself to us by giving ourselves generously to God and our fellow human beings. What could be more reasonable ("logical" in Paul's Greek)? We participate in the gracious order of peace that Christ has inaugurated by being gracious ourselves, gracious to God and gracious to one another. Grace—self-giving love—is to be the standpoint of our moral outlook. It's where we stand; it's the position from which we now occupy our perspective on living.

Then Paul issues a warning. We're terribly liable to absorb our ways of thinking about our world and ourselves from the culture that surrounds us. We are, after all, immersed in that culture. Why do we need to be warned against it? Because our surrounding culture is somehow contrary to the gospel idea of giving. How easy and natural and safe it is just to blend in, to think the way the others do, to adopt (or, perhaps more insidiously, adapt to) their moral outlook, the spirit of this age. None of the moral outlooks in the cultures that surrounded the Roman believers, and none in the cultures that surround us in the twenty-first century, has the standpoint that Paul developed in the first eleven chapters of Romans. None sees the world with eyes fundamentally oriented by generosity. It's easy to let our minds take on the transactional, self-centered form of their minds. It's a way of thinking that we're prone to absorb without thinking. No: we are not to be *con*formed to the present age, but to be *trans*formed by the renewing of our mind. The root "new" in Paul's word "re*new*ing" is the same one that he uses to speak of putting on the new self or human being (Eph 4:24) and taking off the old. The old self is the one that needs to be transformed by learning to think in the way that marks the new age that Christ has inaugurated.

Paul speaks of the renewing of the *mind* (*noûs*). In English editions of Aristotle, this word is translated "the understanding" or "the intellect." It's a capacity to think and reason. It's the seat of the "intellectual" (as contrasting with the "moral") virtues. Paul is saying that our thinking and reasoning, our understanding of life, needs to be renewed so that *we*—our character, our dispositions—will be conformed to Christ rather than to the patterns of the present age. Another word for mind, one that is used in the New Testament about five times as frequently as *noûs*, is *kardia* (think cardiac). It's almost always translated "heart," but it too is a capacity for thinking. For example, "And Simeon blessed them, and said to Mary his mother, 'this baby is destined to be the falling and rising of many in Israel, and a sign of contradiction ... so that the thoughts [reasonings] out of many hearts will be revealed'" (Luke 2:34–35).

Many years ago, a friend of mine was in love. The young woman in question (let's call her Ellie) had professional aspirations. My friend (let's call him Chad) wanted to marry Ellie. She had cooled on him, but was tenderhearted and didn't want to make him feel bad. She somehow made out that her professional aspirations were inconsistent with marrying Chad, and that her aspirations were *rational*. So she spoke of having to obey her "head" rather than her "heart." It was a way of saying "I do love you, Chad, and want (in my heart) to marry you, but I can't because I have to follow my thinking part instead." As I remember, Chad was somewhat comforted by the thought that at least Ellie's irrational part was with him. But he was still pretty miserable.

Like Ellie, some people think the heart and the mind don't intersect. You think with the mind, but you feel and desire with the heart. Each part just does its own thing. The mind is governed by logic and reasoning, but the heart is impulsive and irrational, unless it's kept under control by reason. Plato seems to promote this picture in some passages in his writings, but his considered view is better than this. It is also not the view of Aristotle, who says that good choice of actions requires both correct thinking and correct desiring, and he writes in a way that suggests an intimate integration of reason and desire (see *NE* 6.2).

This is common sense: we think about what we want. And sometimes, as a result of deliberation, we change our minds—that is, our hearts, what we desire. Some thoughts give rise to emotions: anger, joy, disappointment, and so forth. And emotions contain thoughts. For example, anger is likely to include thoughts of revenge, and joy seems to require the thought of something good.

In the New Testament, both *noûs* (mind) and *kardia* (heart) are powers *both* to reason and have thoughts *and* to form cares, desires, concerns, and emotions. In our present passage (Rom 12:2), the new kind of thinking about life that Paul has explained in the first eleven chapters of the letter is supposed to transform the whole character of Christians. It's supposed to be the basis for what we care about and how we care about it. It's supposed to form us as generous, compassionate, gentle, patient, forgiving people, fullheartedly loving God and hoping passionately for his kingdom. When we absorb the new *way of thinking*, we become new *people*, and that's not just a matter of having new thoughts, but of those thoughts transforming our concerns, our emotions and feelings, and our choices.

WHAT IS LIFE? A LOOK AT TWO OUTLOOKS

Let's have a look inside a couple of people's minds. The sketches I'll present are unusual in some ways. Robbiebud and Donniejohn, as I'll call them, are unusually self-aware, articulate, and honest in revealing their habitual patterns of thought. Most of us are less aware of how we think about life, partly because we're less precise in our thinking about ourselves, and partly because we may be a little ashamed of letting it be known, either to ourselves or to others, how we think about life. For present purposes, it's useful to present Robbiebud as articulate and shameless and Donniejohn as theologically articulate. Another way these sketches are unusual is their stark contrast: Robbiebud is not just a non-Christian, but for the sake of the contrast is almost demonic; while Donniejohn is a Christian. Later in this chapter, we'll look briefly at the mind of a good pagan—Aristotle—and mark some ways his mind differs from a Christian mind. We start with Robbiebud's testimony.

> Other people are very important in my life. They serve to give me pleasure (for example, sexual pleasure). I like them when they're inferior to me. I like having power over them. I like it

when they envy and admire me. Money and wealth serve all these ends, so getting money and wealth for myself is a big goal of my daily life. Many people have less money than I have—a fact that I find delightful. But if I can get poor people to adore me, they will give me little bits of money. Since they're poor, they can't each give me much, but since there are so many of them, their contributions add up! My ability to enjoy these goods of course depends on my staying out of trouble. If I'm in jail or in disrepute in the minds of the people who are to give me pleasures, superiority, power, and admiration, that's very, very bad. (Very bad.) On the other hand, there's no limit to what I'll do, provided that it doesn't get me in trouble or prevent me from getting what I like. Truth is really a scam and a hoax that people use to limit one another's powers and options, so I talk a lot about truth and accuse my enemies of lying. This talk helps me get other people onboard with my agenda. But I know its true meaning. I have no respect for people, either. Not even the people who give me pleasures and money and do my bidding. Really caring about truth and respecting other people for *their* sake is for suckers and losers. It's true, of course, that I often have to make people *think* I'm respectful, at least to them, because otherwise I might lose the goods I get from them. I'm open to defrauding, defaming, and debauching people to get pleasure and power for myself. I'm open to threatening people who are disloyal to me and to destroying people I don't like—but only if I think I can get away with it. I don't always get away with it: sometimes people stand in the way of my pleasures, my superiority, my power, and my reputation. But this, too, can be an occasion for a very great pleasure: getting revenge on them. Even though it's compensatory, my getting even (or even *more* than even!) with people who oppose me is a great good, one of the chief pleasures of my life. Revenge is very sweet! It's an especially delicious part of being a winner!

This is an overview of how Robbiebud *thinks* about life. It's an account of his *noûs*. But it isn't just "intellectual"; it's full of passion, desire, and emotion. I began this chapter comparing the idea of a scenic outlook with that of a moral outlook. I pointed out that from a scenic outlook, you can see a variety of things (towns, steeples, forests, rivers, roads, and so forth) from a particular perspective. Robbiebud's moral outlook also has a variety of things "in view": the good, other people, money, power, pleasure, adversity, truth, success and failure, freedom, and justice, for example. And he has a "perspective" on these things that is markedly different from that of a Christian, who has the *same things* in his moral outlook, but sees them from a different *angle*. Consider now the shape of Donniejohn's mind, his outlook, his *noûs*, how he sees life.

> God is the source of everything and the authority over everything. God created me and everything else, so we human beings are beholden to God for everything we are and have. But in Jesus Christ, God visited us in the most intimate and self-giving way: he became one of us, lived a life of service to us, died for our waywardness, and rose from the dead as the harbinger of the general resurrection and the coming age in which God will be properly recognized and honored by all creation, but especially the human community. The logical response to this grace is gratitude. And being grateful, we want to return to God some token of recognition for his generosity. We

do this by loving and serving others in some way distantly similar to the generosity of our beloved God. For us, other people are precious beings whose well-being and pleasure are worth pursuing for their own sake. It's contrary to our view of others that they be mere means to get things we want for ourselves. It's true that other people provide many services to us, and we do enter into transactions for such services. We do jobs for money and we hire people to do other jobs for us. But people's fundamental value for each of us who think as disciples of Jesus is not their utility—their usefulness to us—but *their* good for *their* sake. We respect them as beings just like ourselves. That's why we try hard not to deceive others but speak the truth to them. Whatever material goods we've accumulated, whatever time and talent and energy and reserves of attention we have command over, is to be shared with others for their good.

I speak of what we are called to and what we endeavor to be. We often fall short of what this gratitude entails. We fall (back) into seeing others as devices of our pleasures, profits, and self-importance. We manipulate them by fudging on truth. Sadly, we sometimes see people as obstacles in the way of our projects and become resentful and hostile and harsh to them. On those who are hostile to us, we feel impulses to revenge. If we stay aware of our indebtedness to God's grace by regular celebration of it and prayers expressing our gratitude, such alienating attitudes make us deeply uncomfortable with ourselves. We then find comfort in reflecting that God's generosity extends to us even as sinners and graciously calls us back from our selfishness, our pride, and our alienation from one another. And so, gradually, we become more consistently grateful and generous, and in consequence, more respectful, compassionate, truthful, and forgiving.

Robbiebud and Donniejohn, having human minds, both have outlooks on life. They have shared with us how life looks from where they "stand." We, too, have human minds, and so we all have an outlook on life, though we may be less articulate than they. And this means that we have *ways of thinking about* and understanding various items or features of our lives. Our ways of thinking about these items of life can be very different from one another. The items include our own identities, other people, money and possessions, truth, good and evil, success and failure, power, and authority. The diverse ways of thinking about these items can be called concepts or ideas: Robbiebud and Donniejohn have different self-concepts, different concepts of other people, different ideas of truth, good and evil, power, and authority. These ways of "seeing" the aspects of our lives can become habitual, deeply ingrained. Our different understandings of such life-items can become ingredients of our character and guide the practices of our lives. Our thinking can become the shape of our character. It can yield very different patterns of joys and disappointments, the occasions on which we feel these and other emotions. For example, Donniejohn, because of his generous outlook, tends to rejoice when others have successes or good fortune, and to be saddened when others are disappointed or have troubles. By contrast, Robbiebud is more likely to envy those who are fortunate and to feel superior when others suffer setbacks that he is able to dodge.

Judging by the conceptual order of the mind of Christ, the thinking about life that orders Robbiebud's mind is twisted and depraved. It's not an order of peace, but an order (or disorder!) of Robbie's tyrannical secret war against all. It is a war because his view of us displaces us as souls and turns us, against our will, into mere devices of his will. It is in reality an offense against us, but the war is secret because he will try to make many of us believe he is our friend and advocate.

Nevertheless, I think we can discern in Robbiebud's mind themes that structure the schema of the mind "of this age," as Paul calls it: the competitiveness, the self-centeredness, the greed, the hunger for power, the willingness to deceive, the contempt for fellow human beings, the delight in getting even. Robbiebud breathes deeply as he swims daily laps in his moral cesspool, and it smells to him like gardenias and roses because the disorder of his mind distorts his perception of the moral stench, the rottenness, the putrid corruption of his mind.

I am uncomfortable with Robbiebud's frank endorsement of the elements of his mind. "If I thought that way," I think to myself, putting it mildly, "I'd be ashamed of myself." But of course, I wouldn't, any more than Robbiebud himself does. Like him, I would glory in my shame, because my heart would be formed like Robbiebud's. He is in his element, immersed in this filth because (1) he inhabits the concepts of his mind; they are where he *lives*, they are the terms in which he embraces and practices his life; and (2) he is comfortable with them, in part, because they are the terms in which he cares about things. The cesspool in which he swims smells like gardenias and roses because it defines his *good* as he conceives and desires and practices it. But if there's something better in us, we're uncomfortable with the "body of death" that we perceive in ourselves (Rom 7:24). Even if we're not very deeply catechized in the mind of Christ, we get whiffs of the stink that rises from the surface of the moral cesspool. So we don't glory in our shame as

Robbiebud does, but recoil from it. He's *all* in, but we're just enough in to be mighty uncomfortable.

Donniejohn expresses this discomfort in the second paragraph of his testimony. In his reflections on himself and his philosophy of life he detects a whiff of the spirit of Robbiebud that infects his own spirit. But his attitude about this attitude differs from Robbiebud's attitude about his own. Donniejohn's attitude to his attitude is dismay. Christians call it "contrition" or "penitence," and this, too, is a kind of virtue—a virtue that is special to sinners, and therefore is not quite a part of the mind of Christ, but belongs to the split mind of one who has the mind of Christ, but finds in himself the remnants of another and opposed mind.

ARISTOTLE'S MORAL OUTLOOK

For many contemporary thinkers, Aristotle is the model virtue ethicist. But the modern followers of Aristotle don't usually accept Aristotle's moral outlook. Instead, they follow him in making ethics a study of the psychology of the morally mature person, the person who is fit, by character formation, to contribute to a community that is "happy" (*eudaimōn*). But they have a somewhat different idea of the good life, and so they don't endorse the particular formation of that character that is reflected in Aristotle's moral outlook. If they study the virtues, the character traits they study are not quite the ones that Aristotle commends. His way of thinking about self and social world is not their way.

This difference shows up if we compare Aristotle's catalogue of the virtues with that of modern virtue ethicists. The main moral virtues in Aristotle's list are:

- Justice
- Courage

- Temperance
- Liberality
- Good temper
- Practical wisdom
- Magnanimity

Friendship is an important virtuous bond with another individual. Justice is giving people what is due them, whether that be on a standard of equal distribution of goods or on the standard of what people deserve in the way of rewards and punishments. Justice is very basic among the Aristotelian virtues. For example, it affects friendship by prescribing that the parties be equally good or, if one is more mature than the other, that the less mature party love the more mature more than the more mature party loves the less mature one (*NE* 8.7). This seems to us to be an intrusion of justice into a context where it doesn't belong. Because Aristotle believes that some people are fundamentally inferior to others—because, he thinks, they lack the part of the soul that makes choice possible—it is "just" for fully equipped people, like Aristotle and you and me, to use these "natural slaves" as tools for getting things done, on a sort of analogy with farm animals (*Politics* 1.4). Courage is primarily an excellence in repulsing military attacks on one's city-state. Temperance is a disposition of physical appetites—for food, drink, and sex—that conforms to justice. For example, it would be unjust to spouses (one's own or other people's) to have sex with somebody else's spouse. So the temperate person has this desire and this pleasure only with his or her own spouse. Something similar can be said about temperate appetite for food and drink. Temperance, as described in this way, may be acknowledged as admirable; but it may be thought to be a little unrealistic.

Perhaps this is why Paul mentions self-control, rather than temperance, as a fruit of the Holy Spirit (Gal 5:22). (See ch. 8 of this book.)

Nicholas Wolterstorff has argued that the idea that every human being, just by being human, has an inherent right to just treatment first emerged in the Old and New Testaments, where the rationale for attributing that right to everybody was God's love for everybody.[1] That idea is fundamental to the Christian outlook and belongs to the transformation of our mind that Paul refers to in Rom 12:2. Were Aristotle's mind to be transformed as Paul directs, this would be a change that implies other changes throughout the outlook.

Liberality corresponds to what we would call generosity, but it's different in attitude. Both involve giving away something of value, but generosity is openhanded for the sake of the *other*, while liberality is an expression of the *giver*'s abundance: giving without owing is *largesse*, and it feels good to be large. This strong sense of one's own greatness is most evident in the virtue of magnanimity (literally, having a great soul). The great-souled man has all the virtues and is intensely aware of his own greatness as a human being. He enjoys putting other people in his debt, but dislikes being indebted to others, because it seems to make him less great (see *NE* 4.3). This means that the person of greatest overall Aristotelian virtue is not a grateful person. Gratitude, which is so central in the Christian outlook and so closely connected with generosity, is not a virtue at all in the Aristotelian outlook.

The same can be said of other virtues, such as humility and forgivingness. Humility and gratitude are in tension also with Aristotle's ideal of self-sufficiency. He says that the power of philosophical contemplation (which is an

---

1. Wolterstorff, *Justice*, ch. 5.

intellectual virtue) is greater than the moral virtues because the contemplation of eternal truths can be practiced entirely without physical resources and without anybody else's help (*NE* 10.8). Practical wisdom and the moral virtues that it governs are less great because they depend on a social context and presuppose cooperation, and this dependency undercuts their greatness.

Unlike Aristotle, many modern virtue ethicists *would* count gratitude, generosity, humility, and forgivingness as virtues, though these virtues will not work exactly as they do in classical Christianity. For example, in secular views, a person who feels virtuously grateful for his life wouldn't be grateful to God for it, but might just be "grateful" without being grateful *to* anyone. It might be one of a variety of techniques for reducing your blood pressure. Humility might be defined as an accepting attitude toward your limitations, or as not overestimating your self-worth.[2] Forgiving might be, not a way of loving the one who has hurt you, but a self-focused and self-helping way of freeing yourself from the poison of your own anger. (See ch. 7 of this book.) The inclusion of these "Christian" virtues in secular outlooks might be seen as a credit to the power and attractiveness of Christian ethics, along with a resistance to the central message on which the virtues turn.

CONCLUSION

In this chapter we've tried to get clearer on the role of "big thinking" in the shaping of our character. Big thinking is outlook, overview, worldview, framework. It's a set of ideas that guide and organize the whole mind and heart of the virtues (or the vices, as the case may be). I have suggested that the set of concepts that govern and shape a moral outlook

2. See Whitcomb et al., "Intellectual Humility."

Virtues and Moral Outlooks

are not pre-fixed for us human beings. We might have the outlook that shapes Robbiebud's mind, though most of us will find that shape grotesque and even horrifying. Christians will feel that he is going against his nature as a being who was created for love. Robbiebud's "life" is perversion and vice—not life, but a kind of spiritual death. By Christian standards, we will feel that what we are intended to be has a shape much more like Donniejohn's mind. But I think we can see, too, that the mind or outlook of the Aristotelian is viable in a certain crippled way. Historically, many people, including many in the church, have lived "decent" lives framed with some features of the Aristotelian way. Even some very secularized people now recoil from Aristotle's elitism and exalting of self-sufficiency, though I think in honesty we must admit the Aristotelian tendencies of our own minds. As Paul suggests in Rom 12:2, a significant part of our struggle to be and remain Christians in character and to grow more fully mature as human beings is to be vigilant about the concepts that govern our thinking about God, ourselves, creation, and our fellow human beings.

Much of the thought that formed the minds of the most exemplary characters in the Bible is contained in the Jewish law. How is the law related to the mind of Christ that Paul says we Christians possess? And what do the ordinances of the law have to do with Christian virtues? That's our topic for chapter 4.

FOR DISCUSSION

1. How is a moral outlook like a scenic outlook? How do they differ?

2. Explain why the apostle Paul warns his readers in Rom 12:1–2 about letting their minds be conformed to "this age." What transformation of our minds does Paul

recommend, and what does it imply about our virtues? What does Paul think a "mind" is?

3. How well do the minds of Robbiebud and Donniejohn illustrate Paul's thought?

4. How is Aristotle's idea of eudaimonia related to the biblical idea of shalom (the kingdom of God)? How do these different ways of thinking about the human good affect one's thinking about the virtues?

Chapter 4

VIRTUES AND THE LAW OF GOD

INTRODUCTION

THE LAW OF GOD is a rule of order, a prescription, a standard, a blueprint, a map, a sketch, an outline, a perspective, a guide. A standard, blueprint, map, and sketch, *of what*? Of success in living a human life. An order and rule and prescription *for what*? For happiness. A perspective *on what*? On flourishing as human beings. A guide *to what*? To happiness and well-being for people, to living a good life. "I will never forget your commandments, because by them you give me life" (Ps 119:93).

In the Bible, the body of thought about human living that is called the law (*torah*) is couched in terms of commandments (for example, the Ten Commandments, among many others), though in Jewish tradition the Law (the Torah) is also the name for the first five books of the Bible, which is not just commandments. It also includes narratives and parables, metaphors, and other poetic devices for combatting sin and teaching faithfulness. All that together is the "Law," or "Teaching," and the whole thing is a guide to true life. Thus, commands are only one aspect of the "law."

Nevertheless, let's begin by thinking about commands. I'll propose that the ultimate purpose of the central biblical commands is character formation: a set of traits of excellent, mature, free, and fully functioning human beings.

WHAT IS A COMMAND?

A command is an imperative sentence addressed to someone who is capable of complying with it. It specifies an action or attitude, which it presents as required or prohibited. For example, if the command is "You shall not bear false witness," it specifies an action—telling a lie about somebody—and rules against it. If the command is "You shall not covet," it specifies an attitude—desiring what is someone else's—and rules against it. If the command is "You shall honor your parents," it specifies an attitude *and* its expression in actions—being loyal to your parents and defending their interests—and commends them. In Jesus's comments on the law in Matt 5, he seems to suggest that even the commands that seem to be merely about actions, for example, "You shall not murder" should be read as covering also the attitudes that typically go with the actions: in the case of murder, it rules out ill will: anger, resentment, and hatred. And the reverse seems true too: I think we can infer that where an attitude is commended or prohibited, actions that would express that attitude are also commended or prohibited. For example, "You shall not covet" and "You shall not steal" seem to address two aspects of the same issue: How shall I conduct myself in relation to what belongs to others?

The one who issues the command gives it for a reason. The command expresses a concern on the commander's part. If God commands us to honor our parents, we can be sure that God wants us to have the kind of relationship with our parents that entails honoring them. And more broadly, God wants us to live the kind of life and participate in the kind of social order that is fostered by families in which the children honor their parents and parents give their children what they need for growth in virtue. God, the commander, supposes that, by our obeying that command, we will satisfy such concerns as these. According to Moses, in issuing the commandments of the law, God expresses the concern that his people live the kind of life for which he designed us, a life of peaceful and happy relations (Deut 30:5-6). Apparently, Moses thinks it's important for the people to understand God's purpose in giving them the law: without such understanding, their actions would not be as fully in accord with God's will as God wants them to be. For example, the people might not be grateful to God for the law in the way they may be if they know that God gives it to them for their own good.

Commands can be highly particular: "Shut *that* door *now*!" But the commandments of the law are not like that. They are general; they say: *as a policy*, worship only the true God, *always* honor your parents, and don't *ever* murder or bear false witness or commit adultery. Such *kinds* of action and omission are ruled in, and their contraries are ruled out. This generality of the commandments, along with the importance of the attitudes that characterize the prohibited or enjoined actions, matches the generality of the virtues and the generality of shalom as a patterned way of life. The virtues and the way of social life that they support aren't one-time episodes, but *dispositions* of persons and *patterns* of a way of life.

Since the commandments commend ongoing policy or attitude, moral commandments can be thought more deeply to commend virtues, which combine readiness to act, attitude (motivation), and understanding. In that case, the best way to keep a moral commandment is to have a bent of mind of conformity to it. That way, (1) the outcome is most reliable; (2) the motivation, and thus the action or attitude, is the proper one; and (3) in understanding the command and its reasons, the agent is fully engaged in the action or attitude, and more fully engaged than she would otherwise be with the mind of the commander.

THE RESPONDER

The ones to whom the command is addressed may know and share the commander's concern, and so may obey gladly. On the other hand, they may know the concern and not share it. Consider Robbiebud from chapter 3, whose concerns don't coincide at all with God's concerns in issuing the Ten Commandments. Robbiebud's testimony reveals that his outlook poises him to violate every one of the Ten Commandments. True, we can imagine Robbiebud, under some circumstances, complying (in a way) with a commandment, but doing so for his own reasons of self-protection or glory and not because he shares the commander's outlook. Because such compliance would involve an attitude contrary that of the commander, even this compliance would violate the commandment. Spiritually, keeping a commandment entails being of one mind with the commander.

It's also possible that the responder doesn't know what the commander's concern is or misunderstands it. Imagine a legalist who thinks that "You shall not murder" means only that you shall not cause anybody's body to stop functioning. Jesus says:

> You have heard that it was said to those of ancient times, "You shall not murder"; and "whoever murders shall be liable to judgment." But I say to you that if you are angry with a brother or sister, you will be liable to judgment; and if you insult a brother or sister, you will be liable to the council; and if you say, "You fool," you will be liable to the hell of fire. (Matt 5:21–22)

Jesus is here clarifying the commandment by explaining more fully what the commander (God) has in mind. God wants us not even to act in ways that are similarly hostile to one another, like threatening each other and calling each other names. All of that is prohibited in "you shall not murder."

If we don't understand what the commander has in mind in commanding something, we may think we're obeying it when we're not. The concern to head off this kind of misunderstanding is, I think, behind a lot of the teaching of Jesus and the apostles (especially Paul) about the law. And ultimately, obedience to God's law requires that we wholeheartedly share the concern that moves God to command what he commands. Our reasons need to approximate his. That's part of what it means to love God with your whole heart and mind: you share God's outlook on living; you wholeheartedly endorse it and seek to act on it because you agree, emotionally, that what God commands is good. It gives you pleasure and what is contrary to it repulses you. This oneness of mind is peace with God, just as oneness of mind with fellow church members is peace with them, as Paul suggests in Phil 2:1–2.

Oneness of mind with other people is compatible with disagreeing on particular points. It presupposes the variants of love: gentleness, patience, forbearance, forgivingness, humility, and so forth. In exhibiting these virtues, parties are of one mind that *God's will and the well-being of the people have priority.* In other words, *the thinking of the summary of the law*—"You shall love the Lord your God with all your heart, and with all your soul, and with all your mind" and "You shall love your neighbor as yourself" (Matt 22:37, 39)—*is to be the thinking on which the people are to agree.* This is to be their "mind." The summary of the law, after all, is a statement of the essence and purpose of all the detailed commandments. The thinking of the summary structures these virtues.

In desiring that we obey God's law, Jesus and the apostles want us to have the dispositions of heart that spontaneously incline us to keep the law. In the case of the commandment concerning false witness, the virtues would be truthfulness (truth serves love) and gentleness (anticipatory compassion for the person about whom we bear witness; this especially if the truth we tell is distressing). If the key to understanding the commandment is the love of neighbor, then the prohibition against telling falsehoods about the neighbor is not just that it would be unfair to him to tell a *falsehood* about him, but a more general prohibition against harming him by telling. In that case, it would also rule out telling a hurtful *truth* about him (as gossip often is), unless an overriding consideration favors telling that truth. In the case of the commandment prohibiting murder, the virtues would be compassion and forgivingness—forgivingness to exclude the anger and compassion to the person we might hurt by an expression of anger. If we feel some anger threatening our forgivingness and compassion, then self-control will come into play as a backup. These virtues are the writing of the commandments on our hearts.

RULES ARE UNAVOIDABLE

So it's unsurprising that Paul, who in some way opposes law to grace (Eph 2:15), also says that "obeying the commandments of God is everything" (1 Cor 7:19) and "the law is holy, and the commandment is holy and just and good" (Rom 7:11). Any coherent activity has to be regular (Latin *rego*: to guide, to direct), that is, guided by rules (*regulae*). For example, the idea of a language that has no rules of grammar or syntax or consistent meanings of words is incoherent: such an unmanageable chaos isn't a language at all. If it's to be a *language*, it *must* have a grammar. The grammar needn't be written down, as in a grammar book. It doesn't need to be completely rigid. There's room for saying things that have never been said before. In human living, likewise, there is room within the moral law to do things that have never been done before.

If you speak English as a native speaker, you seldom consult a grammar book (the written code) to speak or write. The grammar is *in you*, ordered by the grammar in your bones. It's a know-how that comes out spontaneously in your activities of speech and understanding of speech. A person who had internalized the law of God as thoroughly as you've internalized the rules of English would have real human life, eternal life, the life of shalom, the life of heaven, a holy life, a righteous life.

FREEDOM, BONDAGE, AND THE LAW

Paul writes:

> For you were called to freedom, brothers and sisters; only don't use your freedom as an opportunity for self-indulgence, but serve one another with love. For the whole law is summed up in a single commandment, "You shall love

your neighbor as yourself." If, however, you bite
and devour one another, look out that you don't
squander yourselves by doing so. (Gal 5:13–15
NRSV modified)

Paul warns the Galatians that in quarrelling with one another, resisting and opposing one another, and being uncivil to one another, they risk wasting themselves on what isn't really life. On the contrary, to live freely as human beings is to give ourselves to one another in love. Freedom of life in Christ is found in the harmony of the community, the good fellowship of mutual gracious giving and receiving, an order of peace.

Freedom is the contrary of bondage—being bound, restricted, impeded—in our ability to act. We can distinguish two kinds of bondage that involve the law of God. One is being in violation of the law. Here, to keep the law is to escape from bondage. The law liberates us to be what we really are, to live a real human life, life that "works" for beings like us. Moses declares this to be the purpose of the law (Deut 30:1–6). Paul acknowledges this when he notes that the whole law can be summed up in the commandment, "You shall love your neighbor as yourself" (Gal 5:14, quoting Lev 19:18). Since the law itself enjoins love and love is freedom, keeping the law is freedom. Psalm 19 celebrates this freedom.

Imagine a person who works in a type of endeavor for which he isn't by nature suited. He labors at this work, perhaps for years, not realizing that temperamentally he's not cut out for it. Work is laborious, and he supposes that that's just the nature of work! Like many others, he greets Friday afternoon with glee and Monday morning with glum. Then, let's say by happenstance, he ends up doing some work for which he *is* well suited. Maybe he moves from business administration to teaching (or vice versa). He starts experiencing joy in his work. All at once he's throwing himself into it, not wanting to stop at the end of the day, and creatively finding good ways to do the work. He feels as though chains have fallen from his arms and legs: he's free! Free *from* burden, and free *to* act. Freedom here is a kind of flow between a person's nature and his activities of living.

The freedom we gain from keeping the law is like this. The law of God is designed for us human beings, to guide us in a life that befits our nature. Just as a tree "demands" water, a human life "demands" the guidance of the law (Ps 1). The law-abiding life is the good life for us because it allows our life to flow naturally, in accord with its deepest natural predispositions. When we live in reverent obedience to God and love for one another, we're living the life that suits a being of our nature. It "works" for us, and living it is freedom.

But it frees us from this kind of bondage only if it has given shape to our concerns, preferences, and dispositions. In metaphors from the prophets, it needs to be "written on our hearts" (Jer 30:31) or digested in our stomachs: "He said to me, Mortal, eat this scroll that I give you and fill your stomach with it. Then I ate it; and in my mouth it was as sweet as honey" (Ezek 3:1–3).

> Your words were found, and I ate them,
> and your words became to me a joy
> and the delight of my heart. (Jer 15:16a)

If we haven't digested the law into our own spontaneous understanding of ourselves and our world, our own desires and aspirations, then it will strike us as an external imposition, a bunch of unwelcome limitations on our freedom. The contrary freedom is the virtues. They are the healthy body that is produced by digesting the law of God.

PART ONE: INTRODUCTION TO VIRTUE ETHICS

VIRTUES AND LEGALISM

Legalism is a kind of myopia: "What forest? I don't see any forest. All these trees are in the way!" It's a bit like a person standing on one of those scenic outlooks, but he's so nearsighted that he sees clearly only the railing that's preventing him from falling into the valley below. The landscape as a whole, with its villages and rivers, fields and forests, is just a blur. So he gets preoccupied with the texture and construction of the railing and misses the essential thing, the outlook. The person with better vision sees the landscape in the perspective afforded by the scenic outlook. In a similar way, the wise reader of the law can use it to get a sense of the moral landscape. And the "vision" that allows him to do so is that the law has been written on his very own heart. The eyes of his heart have been trained in the relative *importance* of the items in the landscape: he knows and feels why it's important to love God, to worship only God, to honor his nearest of kin, and not to steal or slander or commit adultery. And because he's deeply onboard with these things, he makes wise choices from a heart that has been cultivated, under the guidance of the law, to care about what's important.

Legalism isn't the only way to misunderstand the law. The word "antinomianism" is a mouthful that derives from Greek words for "law" (*nomos*) and "opposed" (*anti-*). An antinomian is a person who is opposed to the law. The legalist thinks that the letter of the law is everything, but the antinomian thinks that, because legalism is so myopic, we should ignore the law—letter, meaning, and all. Antinomianism is sometimes commended in Christian circles by appealing to the idea that believers in Christ have been freed from the law. While the apostle Paul does clearly teach that we've been freed from the law in *some* sense, he also makes it clear that in Christ the law has been *fulfilled*, not abolished, and that in clinging to Christ in faith, in the fellowship of his Holy Spirit by which we bear his fruits, we are clinging to a Lord who honors and represents the law in its essence.

KEEPING THE LAW: A MATTER OF LIFE...

I noted in the last chapter that the Bible has a rich concept of what it is to be alive for a human being. The Bible distinguishes life that is death ("you were dead in your trespasses and sins") from life that is really life—life that is truly fulfilling for a human being. "But God, who is rich in mercy, out of the great love with which he loved us even when we were dead through our trespasses, made us alive together with Christ" (Eph 2:1, 4–5). Jesus says, "I came that they might have life, and have it abundantly" (John 10:10). He spoke to them, saying, "I am the light of the world. Whoever follows me will never walk in darkness but will have the light of life" (John 8:12). The light of true human life is the character and friendship of Jesus, which are reflections of the law of Moses.

In Deut 30, Moses identifies the purpose of the law that he has expounded earlier in the book:

> The LORD your God will bring you into the land that your ancestors possessed, and you will possess it; he will make you more prosperous and numerous than your ancestors. Moreover, the LORD your God will circumcise your heart and the heart of your descendants, so that you will love the LORD your God with all your heart and with all your soul, so that you may live. (Deut 30:5–6, with a small change)

Living a human life is made up of many kinds of activities: *interactions with people* of different kinds: spouse, siblings, children, colleagues, clerks, hired hands, employers, strangers; *property transfers*: gifts (giving and receiving), sales, purchases, earning, spending, loaning, borrowing; *knowledge acquisition and transfer*: study, teaching, testimony (receiving and giving); *directing, following, coordinating* (leadership roles, contributions to common projects); *worship*: praise, thanksgiving, confessing, honoring, obeying, adoring; *working and resting*; and so forth. Living consists of such activities. Each of them has ways it is conducted. The law of God covers all these things, in principle. That's why you find such great elaborations, as in the Old Testament books of the Law, rabbinic legal theory, and Muslim legal theory: it can get very detailed and complicated, with detailed elaborations of laws, discussions of exceptions, and possible conflicts among ordinances. Secular laws can also get very complicated; we even have specialists called lawyers and judges. Is there any principle in all this? Does a single aim govern the regulations that govern living? Our minds seek a principle, a unifying and simplifying understanding: what's the point of all this regulation? Arguably, both in the law of God and in secular law, what ties all this together and makes sense of it is something like the good life, the life of shalom.

When legal thinkers get too far into the weeds, we tend to lose sight of the goal. Let's try snapping a wide-angle picture of the good life—shalom—that is envisioned in the law of God.

True life for a human being has two distinct but intersecting "social" dimensions. One is "vertical," the other "horizontal." The living person is in touch with her creator. She knows herself to be under his authority and in his care. His authority is entirely benevolent and his presence surrounds and sustains her on all sides. She loves him with her whole heart and trusts him implicitly. She wants nothing more than to be in his presence and to serve him in all that she does. She praises him for his greatness and thanks him for his goodness to her and to the rest of his creation. The service that expresses her love to him is largely service to his creatures. With a benevolence that reflects the benevolence of God, she tends to the earth, but first to its human inhabitants and above all to those in her immediate surroundings. She is generous to her neighbors with something like the generosity that she receives gratefully from God. She forgives as she has been forgiven; she does what she can to relieve the suffering of fellow human beings. Her heart implies that she has no idols. She reveres God's name, rests in her trust of him, honors the people who have authority over her and over whom she exercises authority, avoids harm to her fellows, keeps her commitments, respects others' property, and is careful to tell only the truth as she knows it. This is her character, the style and spirit of her life.

To live in a social order all of whose participants have this character and live this life of loving God and their neighbors is *shalom*: peace and well-being, the fullness of life. It is what the Bible calls eternal life, the kingdom of God. It is the life of which Jesus is the light. And it is the life that is in full, heartfelt compliance with the law of God.

. . . AND DEATH: A MONKEY WRENCH IN THE WORKS

When someone legitimately requires us to do or not do something or to take a particular attitude, we are, as we say, "under" his authority to comply. When we are indebted to someone for something, we are "under" obligation to pay our debt. We are in a one-down relation with the authority or creditor. Something in human nature resists commands and commandments, debt and duty. We don't like to be told that we *have to* do something, or that we *must not* do something. Some philosophers, including Aristotle, even resist the idea that gratitude is a good thing, because it's an admission of debt and therefore of inferiority (*NE* 4.3). Ralph Waldo Emerson says that if you do someone a favor, brace yourself: "It is a great happiness to get off without injury and heart-burning, from one who has had the ill luck to be served by you. It is a very onerous business, this of being served, and the debtor naturally wishes to give you a slap."[1] And Paul comments that "if it had not been for the law, I would not have known sin. I would not have known what it is to covet if the law had not said, 'You shall not covet.' But sin, seizing an opportunity in the commandment, produced in me all kinds of covetousness. Apart from the law sin lies dead" (Rom 7:7–8). Commands spark rebellion.

Ogden Nash puts the point colorfully in "Kind of an Ode to Duty":

> O Duty,
> Why hast thou not the visage of a sweetie or a cutie?
> Why displayest thou the countenance of the kind of conscientious organizing spinster
> That the minute you see her you are aginster?
> Why glitter thy spectacles so ominously?
> Why art thou so different from Venus
> And why do thou and I have so few interests mutually in common between us? . . .
> Above all, why dost thou continue to hound me?
> Why art thou always albatrossly hanging around me? . . .
> O Duty, Duty!
> How noble a man should I be hadst thou the visage of a sweetie or a cutie!

---

1. Emerson, "Gifts," para. 4.

Nash's poem sounds like doggerel, but it has some pedigrees. It satirizes Wordsworth's "Ode to Duty" and refers to Coleridge's "Rime of the Ancient Mariner" where the albatross, which guides sailors to safety, having been shot dead by the ancient mariner, is hung around his neck. And, I think, Nash's poem is interpretable as deeply Pauline. His character occupies a death- or sin-oriented perspective on life, as do some parts of Rom 7: "Who will deliver me from this body of death?" The difference between Paul and the Nash character is that the latter is a nearly full-time occupant of the sin perspective, while Paul remembers it, but from the perspective of faith in Christ.

Nash exaggerates an attitude that tends to be associated with the concept of duty: if we see some action or attitude as a duty, then our heart is not quite fully in it. We do want to do our duty, but we don't relish the action we have to take. We don't quite love what is commanded. Unlike the psalmist, we don't say of the commands, "More to be desired are they than gold, even much fine gold; sweeter also than honey, and drippings of the honeycomb" (Ps 19:10), as though the requirements of the law are an unqualified blessing, a pure delight. It's more like going to the dentist: we know it's best, but . . . . The desire to do our duty grips our will, "albatrossly hanging around us." This attitude contrasts with the attitude toward God's commandments for which we sinners pray in the collect for the fifth Sunday of Lent:

> Almighty God, you alone can bring into order the unruly wills and affections of sinners: Grant your people grace to love what you command and desire what you promise; that, among the swift and varied changes of the world, our hearts may surely there be fixed where true joys are to be found; through Jesus Christ our Lord, who

lives and reigns with you and the Holy Spirit,
one God, now and for ever. Amen.[2]

True joys are the ones we heard expressed in the last chapter by Donniejohn. Robbiebud's joys are those of a man whose soul is not just in the throes of death, like the Nash character, but who has killed his soul. The joys themselves—joy in superiority, joy in triumphant exploitation of others, joy in revenge—stink like a swollen rotting corpse.

ARISTOTLE AND MOSES

In the latter half of the twentieth century, virtue ethics arose as a philosophical alternative to the theories of "modern" ethics. One of the earliest proposals was an essay by the Christian philosopher Elizabeth Anscombe (1919–2001) titled "Modern Moral Philosophy." Anscombe noted that modern moral philosophy was dominated by the idea of obligation or duty—what people *ought* to do. The notion of "ought" in morality was thought to be unconditional. It was not the kind of "ought" that we invoke when we say, "If you want the door to stop squeaking, you ought to oil the hinges"—as though, if you don't mind the squeaking, then don't bother to oil them: it's up to you. Instead, the moral "ought" is "categorical." To say "you ought not to murder" is to say that no matter what you want, you *must not* murder people. This "ought" expresses an absolute prohibition. Immanuel Kant (1724–1804) is particularly influential here. He thought that the idea of a categorical imperative (in contrast with hypothetical imperatives like the one about oiling your hinges) was the very foundation of ethics.

Kant thought that the categorical imperative derives from pure practical rationality, but Anscombe said that

[2]. See https://www.lectionarypage.net/YearA/Lent/ALent5.html.

such absolute obligations imply an absolutely authoritative lawgiver, namely God. If she's right about that, then the project of modern moral philosophy can be pursued only on the assumption that God is the source of the moral law. She thinks the modern concern about moral obligation is inherited from the Jewish and Christian understanding of ethics and is a holdover from the Bible. But modern philosophers typically don't want to bring God into ethics. In fact, the whole modern project of ethical theory seems to be to find a way to give ethics "teeth" without God. So they're in a professional crisis, according to Anscombe, whether they realize it or not, and must stop talking about moral obligation.

But what will they talk about if moral obligation is off-limits? Anscombe's bright idea was that we could go back to Aristotle and talk about virtues, sparing ourselves the detour through Judaism and Christianity. She didn't deny that there are Christian virtues, but she did seem to think that the Jewish and Christian ethics is a "law conception," in distinction from Aristotle's, which centers on virtues.[3] In this book, we're exploring a Christian virtue ethics, and so we need to think about the relation the Christian virtues bear to the commandments. I'm arguing that a supposed opposition between Jewish moral thinking and thinking about the virtues is false. Jesus is the fulfillment of the *law*. As we have seen, Jesus taught that the commandments are about more than mere behavior; they're about the dispositions of the heart, our mental and emotional life. The apostle Paul gives an even more detailed rundown of the mindset of persons who cling to Jesus in fellowship with the Holy Spirit of God: faith, hope, love, compassion, generosity, forgivingness, forbearance, thankfulness, humility, self-control, patience, and so forth.

3 Anscombe, "Modern Moral Philosophy," 5.

PART ONE: INTRODUCTION TO VIRTUE ETHICS

The supposed opposition between virtue ethics and an ethics of law is also not supported by an investigation of Aristotle. Aristotle's ethics, too, has a place for laws, and it is roughly the same place that Jewish and Christian ethics has for them. In the final chapter of his *Nicomachean Ethics* (10.9), in transition to his second volume, *Politics*, Aristotle notes that to prepare a population of ordinary people to learn virtue, their conduct must be regulated by appropriate laws, with penalties for deviation from them (remember the "blessings and curses" of Deut 30). Conformity to laws doesn't in itself require virtue, because people may behave correctly to get external rewards or to avoid getting in trouble. Still, the effect of good laws will be to habituate the citizens to virtue-like behavior and so to prime them to acquire virtues.

Aristotle also offers moral psychological observations that will encourage people to be correctly motivated in their virtue-like behavior. For example, he says that people can't be considered to have the virtue of justice unless they take pleasure (joy) in performing just actions. And he says, of virtues in general, that virtuous persons must know what they're doing and perform virtuous actions for the right reasons. These comments parallel Jesus's comments in Matt 5 about how the commandments against murder and adultery rule out not merely bad behavior but also murderous and adulterous thoughts and desires.

CONCLUSION

I've proposed that the ultimate function of God's law in the economy of the Christian life is to provide a framework of thought about living freely as a fully human being. If so, then it is to be the shape of a Christian's understanding of living, and thus of his or her mind or heart. And if this is so, the law is the thought that gives characteristic form to the Christian's faith, hope, love, gratitude, generosity, forgiving spirit, self-control, patience, forbearance, boldness, compassion, gentleness, kindness, truthfulness, justice, loyalty, joy, peace, humility, and wisdom.

In part 2 of this book, by exploring the inner workings of these virtues, we will turn to the heart of virtue ethics as we have been conceiving it. But before we do that, in the next chapter, we must take a look at a rather different enterprise that goes by the same name. In fact, it is what comes to the mind of most philosophers today when they hear the words "virtue ethics."

FOR DISCUSSION

1. Why is it important, in keeping God's commandments, to understand God's concern in issuing them?

2. What is it for a commandment to be "written on your heart"? What is the ultimate purpose of the law and how does this purpose get implemented?

3. How is the law a resource of freedom for us human beings?

4. What are legalism and antinomianism, and what's wrong with them?

Chapter 5

VIRTUES AS THE FOUNDATION OF ETHICS

INTRODUCTION

I IMAGINE A PHILOSOPHER who specializes in ethics, and more particularly in virtue ethics. She has read the first four chapters of this book, and she's getting tired and frustrated. "When will Roberts get around to the main topic? When will he get to the important stuff? Doesn't he know what moral philosophy is? When will he finally get to virtue ethics?" What professional moral philosophers expect, under the title of virtue ethics, is moral theory, and so far, we've seen precious little moral theory. I'll point out, in this chapter, that modern virtue ethics is a variant of modern moral theory. It's a different kind of enterprise from what I've been calling Christian virtue ethics. It has a different goal and a different character. What is moral theory?

MODERN MORAL THEORY

The metaphor that guides modern ethical theory is that of an architectural structure—a building—with special attention to its foundation (its "grounding" or "groundwork"). The interest in the foundation is what makes the enterprise philosophical. The ordinary person, "the man in the street," thinks of ethics as answering questions like "Under what conditions is a war just?" "When, if ever, is it OK to abort a living fetus?" "When, if ever, is lying justified?" "Is it moral to redistribute wealth by taxation schemes?" He wants to know the layout of morality. He wants to make his way around inside the building—to be able to find, as it were, the restrooms, the cafeteria, the sleeping quarters, the offices, and so forth. He *lives* in ethics and has some questions about what to do. He respects the building and wouldn't think of hacking his way through a wall for a shortcut to the bathroom or taking the locks off some of the doors so he can sneak into other people's rooms. He just wants to know the arrangement, to accommodate to it and be served by it.

By contrast, the modern philosopher is worried about the foundation. She seems concerned that the whole thing might fall down. If the foundation is crumbly, the whole building is in trouble. If it's not laid on an immovable substratum, the part of the building that people occupy may develop cracks in the walls, the floors may become like hills and valleys, and eventually the whole thing may come crashing down, like the condominium building that collapsed in Surfside, Florida, on June 24, 2021.[1] Ethics as a way of life will become dangerously unhabitable.

The building is a metaphor. It's clear enough what sort of thing the foundation of a building is. You dig down to solid ground, ground that doesn't heave with freezing and

---

1. See "Surfside Condominium Collapse."

thawing or otherwise move; then you pour very hard, rigid concrete with steel rebar to stabilize it even more, and you build the structure on top of that. If all is well done, the building will reliably stay put for years because the foundation won't move, and the building is firmly attached to it.

DESIDERATA OF A FOUNDATION OF ETHICS

But what sort of thing is the foundation of ethics? Modern philosophers have tended to think of ethics as a system of rules: Do this; don't do that. Tell the truth; don't lie. Acquire property by proper procedures; don't steal. Keep your promises. Don't cheat. Treat people fairly. The ethical rules are not singular commands like "pay the electric bill that came to you on October 15, 2026." No, they have generality: "pay your bills"; or even more generally, "pay your debts"; or even more generally, "pay what you owe" or "deal justly." The modern ethical theories are efforts to answer the question, what is the *most* general, the deepest, the most basic, the most indisputable, principle of moral conduct? This, it is thought, would be the principle that supports and governs all the other principles.

Since the structure that is to be supported by the foundation of morals is a set of rules or principles, the notion of *support* is conceptual. It's comparable to the support of a conclusion by premises. The premises of an argument are a basis or foundation of the argument's conclusion. Similarly, the support that the foundational principle of ethics affords to the rest of ethics is something like logical derivation: the less fundamental principles of morality need to *follow from* the foundational principle.

Just as the foundation of a building has to meet requirements about the materials of which it's made and the basis on which it rests and be attached to the building with sturdy bolts and nuts, the foundation of ethics has to meet certain stability-requirements without which it couldn't serve as a foundation and be attached firmly to the more specific moral principles. Note three such requirements.

a. Complete Generality

Moral principles, I noted, are general. But each covers only an aspect of morality, say, property or testimony or promises. Each principle must cover all the cases of its domain, but not the cases of other domains. It has that much generality, but not more. In contrast, the foundation has to support the *whole* of morality. If the foundation of a building weren't under the whole structure, the parts that extended beyond the foundation would be unsupported. Is it conceivable, though, that different parts of a building are supported by different foundations, like a shed that's held up by posts on four corners? The four posts, though separated in space, are the *one* foundation of the shed. Each one has to rest on solid ground, and by their locations, they are *coordinated* as support for the shed. Similarly, some partisans of the moral theory known as intuitionism hold that there are several basic moral principles; but they are held together by the notion of moral intuition, a moral faculty of the human mind. That power of intuition is the ultimate foundation, and it is presented as having the required complete generality.

b. Compelling Appeal

A proper foundation, according to advocates of moral theory, has to be undeniable by rational people. It must not be arbitrary or culturally relative in any way. It has to be so universally compelling that you would have to be quite irrational or perverse to deny its appeal. In chapter 3, I talked about moral outlooks (plural), of which Christianity is one. Christians think that everybody ought to find Christianity appealing, since it's so glorious and we, at least in our best moments, have glimpses of its glory. But in fact, not everybody finds it compelling. So, to the mind of moral theorists, Christian theology doesn't qualify as a foundation of ethics. Any proposal for the foundation of ethics must garner universal adherence, at least among rational people of good will.

As we'll see, different kinds of moral theory propose foundations with different kinds of compelling appeal. Kantians think their favored foundation is indisputable because it's a kind of rationality; utilitarians think that nobody in his right mind could deny that happiness is the good; social contract theorists think we have to agree about the basis of morality because the basis just *is* an agreement; and sentimentalists seem to think that, under certain conditions, our natural emotion-generating dispositions reliably constitute (by a kind of projection) the goodness and badness of things.

c. Basis of Agreement about Moral Issues

One of the prompts for modern ethical theory is the problem of moral disagreement, and moral theory hopes to provide, by its foundation, the means for overcoming disagreement. Moral people disagree about many things. Is it fair to redistribute income by taxation? Some might appeal to the principle that you have a right to keep what you've earned. Others might say it's not fair for a minority of people to have a majority of the wealth. People disagree about whether a woman may sovereignly choose whether to destroy the fetus that's living and growing in her very own body. Some point out that she has a right to control her own body, while others say that the fetus isn't part of her body but has a distinct moral status. Some people think that some businesses should be free to discriminate among customers on the basis of the customers' sexual orientation, while others say that such discrimination violates the rights of customers. A proper moral theory, some philosophers hope, would allow us to resolve these disagreements by appeal to the fundamental principle of ethics.

SOME PROPOSED THEORETICAL FOUNDATIONS

There are roughly four kinds of traditional modern ethical theories. They are Kantian deontology, utilitarianism, social contract theory, and sentimentalism.

a. Kantian Deontology

In his book *Groundwork of the Metaphysics of Morals*, Immanuel Kant (1724–1804) proposes that the foundation of ethics is a quasi-logical principle to the effect that whenever you perform an action it should be such that you can will that the rule enjoining that action be universally obeyed. According to Kant, this is the principle of duty and of "practical rationality": that you be willing that everybody in circumstances like your present ones should follow the rule of your proposed action. Kant calls this "the categorical imperative." I say it is *quasi*-logical, because Kant thinks that if a rule is immoral and you try to will it to be a universal law, you end up contradicting yourself. For example, if you're deciding whether to tell a lie and you try to allow that everybody in your circumstances should lie as you propose to do, you would undermine the whole institution of giving testimony, and so it would become impossible to lie: nobody would trust anybody, and false statements couldn't have the force of lies. Universal lying is a practical contradiction.

Kant seems to think that rationality is so fundamentally appealing or compelling that it's a fit foundation for moral thought. But even if he's right about that, his rule is only quasi-logical, because you can avoid the "contradiction" by declining to universalize. When people lie, they don't necessarily contradict themselves, because they don't will that everybody should lie in the same circumstances. The requirement to universalize isn't characteristic of logic. If you violate a law of logic by saying p and not-p, you contradict yourself whether or not you will that everybody do the same. By contrast, in ethics, it's up to you whether you will the rule you follow to be universally obeyed.

b. Utilitarianism

A rival theory is the utilitarianism of John Stuart Mill (1806–73). Mill proposes that ethics be secured by its foundation in the principle that a person should always choose the course of action that will lead to the greatest happiness for the greatest number of people.

> The creed which accepts as the foundation of morals, "utility" or the "greatest happiness principle," holds that actions are right in proportion as they tend to promote happiness; wrong as they tend to produce the reverse of happiness.[2]

Like Kant's appeal to logic or rationality, Mill's appeal to happiness is intended to elicit universal agreement. What could be more rock solid than the value of happiness? It's uncontroversial: everybody wants it and immediately sees its appeal, right? Of course, there is the little question

---

2 Mill, *Utilitarianism*, ch. 2, para. 2.

about what, exactly, happiness is. On that question, Mill differs from his utilitarian predecessor Jeremy Bentham (1748–1832), who thought that happiness was any pleasure whatsoever, regardless of how "low" it was. Mill thought, to the contrary, that the pleasures of good poetry are better, as pleasures, than the pleasures of a stupid game called push-pin. Aristotle thought that happiness (eudaimonia) was a lot deeper than the pleasures of good poetry and required living in a well-ordered city-state and being well developed in the whole range of virtues.

Despite its name, utilitarianism is not very manageable as anything more than the roughest guess as to what is best to do. It would take the powers of an omniscient supercomputer to figure out the probable happiness-consequences of simple actions for all the persons who are affected by such actions, not to speak of complex questions in international politics.

c. Social Contract Theory

Thomas Hobbes (1588–1679) is the modern representative of social contract theory, though a useful sketch of the idea is found in Plato's *Republic*, book 2, expressed clearly and succinctly by Glaucon:

> The badness of suffering [injustice] so far exceeds the goodness of doing [injustice] that those who have done and suffered injustice and tasted both, but who lack the power to do it and avoid suffering it, decide that it is profitable to come to an agreement with each other neither to do injustice nor to suffer it. (358e–359a)

The agreement that establishes all the moral principles is a trade-off. We agree to abide by the rules in exchange for other people's agreeing to do the same. We all get half (the better half) of what we want: we don't get to do just anything we want, but in exchange, we don't suffer the consequences of other people doing whatever *they* want. Here the principle of the moral principles is the agreement or contract to abide by the principles. Many of us don't remember having signed the contract, but maybe we can be thought to have agreed to it implicitly by accepting the benefits of having the rules. But then we might think that the argument commits the fallacy of begging the question: the agreement can't be the foundation of morality if you have to be moral to abide by the agreement.

We might think also, with Socrates, that the attitude expressed in the compromise of this agreement isn't really morality, but a kind of cynical self-serving. The main burden of Plato's dialogue, *Republic*, is to show that moral rectitude, the life of justice, is desirable "for its own sake," that is, *intrinsically good for human beings*, and is not, as the social contract theory suggests, just a cagey strategy for getting something else—namely, as much advantage as possible for ourselves.

d. Sentimentalism

The fourth kind of moral theory is sentimentalism. The most famous advocate of this theory is David Hume (1711–76). Hume's theory trades on the fact that the most basic way we perceive the goodness of things is by our "positive" emotions (joy, hope, gratitude—in short, pleasure) and the badness of things by our "negative" emotions (fear, anger, sadness—in short, distress). Moral principles all have the character of attributing worthiness of approval to some class of actions and situations (say, just, kind, generous ones) and worthiness of disapproval to some other, contrary class of actions and situations (say, unjust, cruel, and stingy ones). So the origin of all moral distinctions, according to sentimentalism, is human sentiments. They are the "principle" of all the principles. The sentiments (emotions) are the foundation of ethics.

What is a sentiment? For the sentimentalist, it seems to be a disposition to develop emotional dispositions. A sentiment is not an emotion, but an innate tendency or readiness to have emotional experiences of a certain pattern. Hume speaks, for example, of the "sentiment of humanity" as the basis for such virtues as generosity and gentleness. The sentiment of humanity is the natural tendency to develop a concern for other people such that we enjoy seeing people who are happy and prosperous, and dislike seeing people who are miserable and struggling to survive. If, as we've been arguing in this book, these virtues are modes of caring for people, then the sentiment of humanity would be our innate human tendency to develop these modes of caring. The fact that infants in the crib sometimes cry in response to other infants crying (a response reminiscent or anticipatory of compassion) betokens the sentiment of humanity. There might also be a sentiment of justice, a natural readiness to come to value fairness. But in addition to such innate dispositions to develop the virtues, we must admit that we have sentiments that are the basis of vices: of selfishness, of cruelty, and of envy. Of these, too, we see evidence in very young children. If sentiments are to be the foundation of morality, then sentiments will be also the foundation of immorality: of joy in others' suffering (cruelty), of distress at others' success (envy), and of indifference to the prosperity and well-being of others (stinginess, vaulting ambition). If sentimentalists base morality on the fact that moral sentiments are natural to the human constitution, they will also need to rest immorality on the *same* foundation. A foundation of morality shouldn't be indifferent toward the distinction between morality and immorality, but sentimentalism's foundation doesn't seem to favor morality. Furthermore, it doesn't follow from the fact that emotions are the most complete way to *perceive* moral values (making sentiments crucial to their perception) that emotions *create* moral values (and are therefore the *basis* of moral values).

e. Divine Command Theory?

Some theists (such as Robert Adams and Phillip Quinn) have proposed what they call a divine command theory. A complete divine command theory would say that the foundation of *all* of ethics is God's will, which is expressed in his commandments. However, the most thoughtful versions of this theory claim less than this, saying that divine commands are foundational only for the area of ethics having to do with obligations. There is more to moral thought than obligations. There is also the good. Utilitarianism offers an account of the good, namely human pleasure and absence of pain. Aristotle has a more complex view, according to which the human good is a virtuous social life that he calls eudaimonia. We've seen that Christian ethics says that the good is an order of peace in which God is worshiped as God and fellow humans are loved as brothers and sisters.

If a divine command theory gives only an account of obligation, then it lacks the complete generality that a moral theory requires. But it also lacks the universal appeal needed for resolving, in a final way, disagreements about more particular moral questions. Not everyone believes in God or has the same conception of God and God's commands, so to try to resolve moral disputes by pointing out what God commands or prohibits is not a good general strategy for resolving moral disagreements.

Jesus cites the commandment that you love God with all your heart and your neighbor as yourself (Matt 22:34–40) and says that on this law "hangs all the law and the prophets." This sounds a bit like a foundation of ethics. But for modern philosophy, "the law and the prophets" of Judaism and Christianity isn't identical with morality as such because it doesn't have the universal appeal, and thus can't serve as a final arbiter of moral disagreements. Many modern people simply deny the authority of the law and the prophets. They might reject the idea that love for God is basic to morality, because they don't think God exists. They might reject the idea of marriage that lies behind the supposition that adultery is wrong. Or they might think that it's perfectly OK to covet (envy) another's property, as long as you don't steal it.

So most philosophers wouldn't include divine command theory as an example of modern moral theory. I will assume, then, that the main moral theories are Kantian deontology, utilitarianism, social contract theory, and sentimentalism. They are the standard philosophical theories about the foundation of ethics—that is, until "virtue ethics" comes along.

VIRTUE ETHICS

I began this chapter by imagining a modern moral philosopher who has read the first four chapters of this book on virtue ethics and complains that I haven't yet said anything about virtue ethics. That philosopher has in mind a variant of modern ethical theory that emerged in the second half of the twentieth century. I mentioned Elizabeth Anscombe's 1958 essay "Modern Moral Philosophy" in which Anscombe proposed that philosophers drop their concern with moral obligation and turn back instead to Aristotle and the investigation of virtues. Another landmark in the recent history of moral philosophy was Alasdair MacIntyre's *After Virtue: A Study in Moral Theory* (first edition 1981) in which he proposed a study of the virtues as a path to resolving the seemingly endless disagreements about moral issues in modern society. Neither of these works makes a very clear case for a moral theory in which the notion of a virtue would occupy the role formerly given to practical reason, the general happiness, a social contract, or innate human dispositions to acquire moral emotion dispositions. That task was left for later, less distinguished thinkers to take up.

On Virtue Ethics by Rosalind Hursthouse is an introductory text that contains the notion of a virtue ethics as a moral theory, but Hursthouse is not consistent in this. For example, she explicitly disavows any suggestion that her version of virtue ethics is foundationalist (making virtues the foundation for all of ethics) or reductive ("reducing" concepts like *duty*, *rights*, and *the good* to variants or implications of the concept of *virtue*).[3] Yet earlier in the book, she says, "According to virtue ethics—and in this book—what is wrong with lying, when it is wrong, is not that it is unjust (because it violates someone's 'right to the truth' or their 'right to be treated with respect') but that it is *dishonest*, and dishonesty is a vice."[4] And she goes on to say that murder is wrong, not because it violates the murdered person's right to life, but because it is callous and contrary to the virtue of charity. This exclusionist "not *x*, but *y*" way of thinking about deriving ethical concepts *is* the foundationalist or reductivist approach. A person who was not committed to virtue ethics as a theory would be open to an inclusive approach allowing a *variety* of reasons for thinking that lying

3. Hursthouse, *On Virtue Ethics*, 82–83.
4. Hursthouse, *On Virtue Ethics*, 6.

is bad practice: it often hurts and disadvantages people, it expresses an alienating disrespect for the persons who are lied to, it undermines institutions like contract-making and people's trust in one another, *and* it is a mental/moral corruption of the liar (that is, a vice). A thinker who isn't treating virtue ethics as a modern moral theory should be open to *all* good reasons to shun lying.

Gary Watson's "On the Primacy of Virtue" is a more consistent presentation of modern virtue ethics. Watson cites John Rawls:

> The two main concepts of ethics are those of the right and the good; the concept of a morally worthy person is, I believe, derived from them. The structure of an ethical theory is, then, largely determined by how it defines and connects these two basic notions.[5]

Kant's moral theory is an example of the claim that "the right" (the concept of our duty) is the foundation of ethics, while Mill's theory illustrates the claim that "the good" is basic, instead. Both of these, as we have seen, reject the idea that virtue ("the concept of a morally worthy person") is basic: each of these classical moral theories takes the concept of virtue to be derivative from their favored concepts: Kant thinks that the concept of virtue derives from the concept of our duty (the right), while Mill thinks the concept of virtue derives from the concept of good (the greatest happiness for the greatest number). For Kant, what makes a person virtuous is the tendency to do his duty, while for Mill, a person is virtuous if and only if he tends to bring a greater balance of happiness into the world.

A virtue ethics, according to Watson, is a third option beyond the classical modern theory that the right is basic

---

5. Rawls, *Theory of Justice*, 74.

and its alternative that the good is basic. Virtue ethics, by contrast, is the view that the right and the good both derive from the concept of virtue. On the ethical theory of virtue ethics, what makes a good action good or a right action right is ultimately that it was performed by a virtuous person acting virtuously—for example, that the good action was performed benevolently (out of the virtue of benevolence) or that the right action was performed dutifully (out of a sense of duty).

Contrary to Rosalind Hursthouse's more irenic, antitheory mood, these three theories are fierce competitors, inveterate rivals, exclusively territorial. Only one thing, according to the theoretical mindset, can be the foundation, as Hursthouse suggests when writing in her "not *x*, but *y*" mood. If virtue ethics is a moral theory, then it rejects the idea that either the good or the right is basic to ethics, and claims that, *instead*, virtue is basic.

Watson seems to assume, in this paper, that having a moral theory is a good thing, or at least that it's the sort of thing that a philosopher of ethics *does*. He seems to follow Rawls in assuming this. But *is* a moral theory a worthy human pursuit? Is it a useful way to spend a philosopher's time? What would justify this activity? Why would anybody think it worthwhile? What is its value?

Earlier modern philosophers like Kant and Mill probably thought that they were guarding human morality by giving it a foundation. They may have thought that, without a firm conceptual foundation of the kind they thought themselves to be laying, the institution of morality might fall apart and become uninhabitable. I doubt that many philosophers who "do" moral theory today seriously believe they're doing any such service. They realize that the proposed theories are far less compelling than the institution—morality—whose foundation the theories are supposed to

Virtues as the Foundation of Ethics

shore up. The debates among the theories' adherents have been going on for well over two hundred years—and they go on and on. All the theories are highly controversial, as the history of philosophy shows—at least as controversial as any of the moral judgments that the theories are supposed to justify. You might be tempted to suspect that for contemporary philosophers, moral theorizing is less a serious moral project than an amusing competition for the display of intellectual subtlety.

That said, moral theorizing does bear some fruits, though not of the kind at which theory ultimately aims (and perhaps not very impressive, for all the intellectual energy expended). Along the way, concepts do get sharpened in the course of thinking and debate. For example, a theory based on the concept of virtues requires some background thinking about the nature of virtues, and perhaps of particular virtues, such as justice, compassion, or courage. Indeed, any theory—whether it be good based, obligation based, or virtue based—needs to have *some* concept of the good, *some* concept of obligation, and *some* concept of virtue, since these are all important moral concepts that would need to be accommodated and explained in any theory. And, though the end goal of theory making may be fatuous, the process can yield useful clarifications.

Here are some examples of insights that arise in the course of theorizing: Watson notes that virtues are qualities that make their bearers good specimens of their kind, whether the kind be *tiger* or *human being*. This is an Aristotelian insight, but it might be prompted by a need to say something clear about what virtue is. Rawls makes many points about the concept of justice that are interesting and valuable quite apart from their roles in his theory, and yet are ones that he might not have made had he not been engaged in the theoretical project. Kant makes the solid

93

conceptual point that you can't have an obligation to do something that you simply can't do. That is a clarification of a basic concept of ethics, and a worthwhile contribution to our understanding of duty. And Mill makes the good point (though it tends to sabotage his utilitarianism) that pleasures don't all have the same value: some are admirable, some trivial, and others despicable. The fact that utilitarians make pleasure (happiness) so central to ethics naturally prompts the utilitarian to try to clarify the concept, and philosophical integrity pushed Mill to see this truth. In Mill's case, the solid insight works against the theory or makes it even more complicated, since his theory presupposes our ability to quantify pleasure across populations and makes the quantity of pleasure the measure of good.

CONCLUSION

Christian virtue ethics isn't a theory. It isn't an attempt to lay a foundation of ethics that compels general assent and from which the ethical concepts derive by compelling logic. Instead, it's an *exploration* of the concepts that shape the Christian mind and heart with special focus on the virtue concepts. The purpose of this exploration is to clarify the ground plan of our moral habitation according to the Christian tradition, and especially the Bible. Christian virtue ethics is not so much about the foundation as it is about the layout of the building. Its purpose is to help us find the rooms—the right room for the right time for the right purpose. Ultimately, its aim is to provide a tiny aid to the thinking that will become the spontaneous form of our heart/mind, making us fit participants in the order of peace that Jesus has promised us.

The discussions that follow, in part 2 of this book, will attempt to make clearer the contours of the Christian virtues that come up here and there in the New Testament, especially in the letters of Paul the apostle. The purpose will be the same as Paul's—to recruit and nurture Christians in the church—though the way of going about it is different. This, it seems to me, is a fitting use of philosophical energy and skill. It is closer to the heart of ethics, the actual living of the ethical life, than the rather remote preoccupation with foundations that usually guides philosophical thinking. It also seems more likely to succeed in its purpose, given the historical evidence of the last two hundred years of philosophical ethics, much of which looks suspiciously like tilting at windmills.

I've tried to keep the chapters of part 2 short. Our tradition offers many virtues to discuss, and each would merit a much longer and deeper discussion than this policy allows. I have tried to make a few of the most important points about each virtue, but the brevity means that I've left out many interesting insights about them. In an afterword at the end of this book I have listed, for the interested reader, some other things I've written that go into richer detail.

FOR DISCUSSION

1. What is modern moral theory? How does it differ from the exploration of moral concepts (for example, virtue concepts) that Roberts commends?

2. Why do some people think it's important to establish the foundation of ethics? What kind of thing is a foundation?

3. Briefly explain each of the four chief modern ethical theories and any objections to them that you can think of.

4. How is modern virtue ethics a variant of modern ethical theory? How does Christian virtue ethics differ from such a theory, according to Roberts?

PART TWO
SOME CHRISTIAN VIRTUES

Chapter 6

FAITH, HOPE, AND LOVE

INTRODUCTION

FAITH, HOPE, AND LOVE are a trio of virtues that the apostle Paul combines in 1 Cor 13 (v. 13), a chapter primarily devoted to the virtue of love for fellow human beings. In this combination, they have been called the "theological virtues," as distinguished from the ancient Greek "cardinal" (*cardo*, Latin for hinge) virtues of justice, temperance, courage, and wisdom. None of the theological virtues is found in Aristotle's ethics, while the cardinal virtues have special prominence. The cardinal virtues are also found in the writings of Plato. In this chapter I will treat faith, hope, and love as theological: as faith in God, hope in God, and love of God. But I will also claim that they imply the "humanistic Christian virtues," as we might call them, which center around variants of the love of fellow human beings. The rest of the chapters of part 2 will consider the humanistic virtues, the virtues that govern human interactions in an order of peace.

The first three of the Ten Commandments (Exod 20:2–7) are also "theological" in telling us how to relate specifically to God. We are to have no other gods than God, we are to have no idols, and we are not to bear (or carry) God's name in vain. Moses summarizes these commandments as "You shall love the LORD your God with all your heart, and with all your soul, and with all your might" (Deut 6:5). These commandments, and all the rest, are an essential element in a covenant that God strikes with the people of Israel.

In the Christian character, the theological virtues form the basis for all the virtues that fit us to live together with our fellow human beings in an order of peace. The theological virtues together form the substance of the mind that is rightly ordered to the covenant that God made with Israel through Moses. In the law, that covenant outlines the life of peace to which God calls us.

Faith is *our trust in God* to give us that life if we keep the law. It is trust in God's trustworthiness for his promises. So our faith assumes God's faithfulness. We depend on it, and this depending is our faith, our faith in God's faithfulness to his covenant with us. Likewise, mutually *God trusts us* to keep the commandments.

But that depending is also hope: we hope, in God, for the order of our peace. And God, in making the covenant, hopes in us. God hopes that we will keep the covenant. He depends on us.

How do we depend on God? *How* do we hope in God? We do so by loving God and loving what God aims at for us. Our covenantal relation to God is like a marriage: it's not just a business deal—if you do this for me, I'll do that for you—but a love relationship in which we are moved to faithful keeping of the promise by our love to the one to whom we are faithful. Conversely, God gives us the law and keeps his side of the deal because he loves us. Accordingly, as Jesus teaches, the "point" of the law is that we be transformed into lovers of God and our neighbor. The personal qualities of such lovers are the virtues. Hope is confident, happy, anticipation of the life of love that is peace with God and neighbor.

COVENANT

Let's think first about faith and hope. When you make a contract with somebody, both of you make it *for* something—some gain or good. Let's say you sign a contract with a builder to build you a house. The house is the good or gain that you hope for in making the contract, and on her side, the builder hopes to make some money on the deal. But you have that hope only if you trust the builder to build a good house for you at the contracted price and she has hope of being paid only if she trusts you to carry through. To have hope that she'll keep the contract, you have to have faith in her. On the builder's side, she has to sign the contract in good faith, that is, in a way that is worthy of your trust. Your faith that she'll deliver assumes her signing the contract in good faith—trustworthily. And she has to have confidence that you, on your side, are good for your promise to pay. Both parties' confidence in hope depends on faith, and the hope is well grounded only if both parties are faithful to the contract, and thus to the other party. Faith is two-way trust. So she and you both have to have faith in one another if you are both to have the hopes that the contract is designed to secure. Otherwise, the contract is worthless. Without the fulfillment of these hopes, the covenant has failed.

PART TWO: SOME CHRISTIAN VIRTUES

In a similar way, God strikes an agreement with the people of Israel. God says, as it were, "Here's the deal. I have some rules I want you to keep, and if you keep them, you'll live well. If you don't, things won't go so well for you." And the people say, "OK, it's a deal." The people agree to abide by the law and God agrees to be their God in a special way, to lead them into a good land, guide them in living, protect them from their enemies, and abide with them as king over them in an order of peace. This is what the people can hope for in their agreement with God. From God's side, God is investing in the prospect that the people of Israel will be *his* in a way that is special among the peoples of the earth. This is God's hope. And, as we learn in the Bible, God hopes that, by way of Israel as a kind of representative, all the peoples of the earth will come to be his in this special way. He will be king over all the earth.

It might seem to some of the people that the covenant was a business deal, like hiring a builder to build you a house. God says if I keep these rules, I'll prosper. I want to prosper, so I'll play by the rules. You agree to pay the money, and the builder makes a house for you. You may not like her very much, but you don't care, as long as you get the house you want. You certainly aren't interested in living the rest of your life with your builder. This is the kind of attitude that seems to be sustained by what is called "the prosperity gospel." We can be rich, healthy, and prominent if we just stay in God's graces. So let's go for it.

But the covenant between God and his people isn't like that. And so we come to love's part in the package of the theological virtues. In the Old Testament, the covenant between God and his people is often likened to the agreement between a man and a woman in which they become permanently coupled, bound to one another with the bonds of trust in one another and faithfulness to one another, a common hope for the future, and love for one another. It's true that each of them gets many good things: help from the other, good times in bed, relief from loneliness, heirs, and so forth. But *in* all that, they get *each other*, and they get the joy of *giving themselves* to each other. Unlike your relationship with your builder, marriage is a bond of *love*. The next time you need a house, it's perfectly OK to go with a different builder. But if you up and decide to get your love from another "spouse," it's called adultery. And it's not OK. Nobody would say that when you go with a different builder, you're being faithless, you're betraying her, and you're a scumbag. But that's what we say about adulterers. This contract is for life, in more than one sense.

In marrying someone, you contract, not just for goods of which the spouse can be your supplier, but for the spiritual good of your spouse's devotion to you and yours to your spouse. You contract for a unique personal relationship with this other person. You offer your devotion to him or her in "exchange" for her or his devotion to you. The word "exchange" is odd in this context, and I put it in quotation marks to indicate that it's not to be taken in its usual commercial sense. You commit *yourself* to love *this person* uniquely as long as you both shall live, and in "exchange," she or he commits for the same to you. It's a personal relationship, a friendship, and more than a friendship.

God is to be the beloved of his people; his people are to love him with all their heart, just as he loves them and wants to be their God and king. This is what the people are promising in "exchange" for God's love. If it is an "exchange" of goods, the goods are selves—the self of the people and the self of God. God wants to "define" himself as the God of Israel, and he wants Israel to define herself, in her fullest understanding, as belonging to him, much as a woman and a man, in marrying, redefine themselves as belonging to each other.

Love is a melding of purpose. You will remember that in chapter 4 we found that to obey a moral command in the deepest sense is to be of the same mind as the commander, to intend, in obeying, what the commander intends in commanding. This sameness of mind is a dimension of love, and again, we see it in the marriage relation. If a marriage develops well, then the two become not only one flesh, but in a sense and no doubt more gradually, one mind. They may disagree about this or that, but they agree, as they agreed aloud at the wedding ceremony, only now much more deeply, on the ends and the means of the union of marriage.

The heart of the covenant is this close and happy relationship between the people and God.

FAITH, HOPE, AND LOVE AS VIRTUES

If faith, hope, and love, as they are understood in the Bible, are virtues, then they are reliable dispositions. People with these virtues are "steadfast." They are undeterred. They stick in place. They hold their ground. And the place they stick is faith, hope, and love. These virtues dispose us to think in certain ways, to care consistently about certain things, habitually to see the "world" in their terms, and to act in ways that accord with this thinking, caring, and perceiving. A traditional term for this reliability of disposition is *habitus*, a Latin word that is often translated, a little awkwardly, as "habit." "Habit" is awkward because habits tend to be mechanical and automatic. "Sorry, I wasn't thinking; I'm just in the habit of doing that." A *habitus*, by contrast, is intelligent and discriminating. For example, an artist's reliable disposition to create beautiful things is a *habitus* (a skill, an ability, a flair, an "art"), but it would be odd to call it a habit. "She's in the habit of making beautiful sculptures" sounds like a joke. But it's not *entirely* wrong to think of virtues as habits because, even if it's a bit mechanical, a habit has that dependability, that predictive character, that grain in the person, that is also true of virtues. And virtues do have a dimension of automaticity. For example, deeply just people spontaneously "see" injustices and recoil, without thinking or trying. They are just that way. But after this initial spontaneity, they may have to think hard and long about what to do about the injustice, and their ability to do so well is essential to their virtue of justice.

In describing the importance of faith and faithfulness to the making of covenants, we have built this reliability into the idea. If our confidence that the builder will carry through on the contract is based on our power to ruin her business if she doesn't, and thus on knowing how much she would be afraid not to keep the contract, then our faith is not *in her*, and her supposed faithfulness is not her trustworthiness, but her fear of retribution. For our relationship through the contract to be one of faith and faithfulness, the two parties need to *be* trusting and trustworthy.

FAILURE OF THE COVENANT

The arc of the Old Testament covenant story isn't happy. Israel, it turns out, is not a reliable covenant partner. Her love fails. She defaults. Starting immediately during the trek from Egypt through the wilderness to the promised land, the people's confidence in God's promises fails, they complain about what God provides for them, and they chase false gods. Later, they demand a human king like other peoples. They are seduced by the supposed divinities of the populations native to the country they're occupying. And the consequences are as predicted: neighboring groups harass them, they are overwhelmed by great powers to the north, Solomon's Temple is destroyed, and eventually the population is carried into exile and back into slavery. By the time of Jesus, Israel is occupied by Rome.

Israel realizes that if she is to have hope, it will need to be by God's forgiveness. Hope, if it is to be sustained, must have a basis other than the people's faithfulness to the covenant. That God is disposed to forgive Israel's faithlessness is a message of prophets such as Isaiah, Jeremiah, and Ezekiel.

FAITH AND HOPE IN THE CONTEXT OF A NEW COVENANT

To facilitate Israel's escape from slavery, God had sent a series of plagues on Egypt, the last of which was the death of the first-born in each Egyptian household. In preparation for this, the Lord had instructed the Israelites to slaughter a lamb on the evening before their flight from Egypt and eat it roasted. "They shall take some of the blood and put it on the doorposts and the lintel of the houses in which they eat it.... The blood shall be a sign for you on the houses where you live: when I see the blood, I will pass over you [thus, the "Passover"], and no plague shall destroy you when I strike the land of Egypt" (Exod 12:7, 13).

On the night before Jesus was betrayed by one of his own disciples (faithful to the pattern of human unfaithfulness), he celebrated the Passover meal with them. "Then he took a cup, and after giving thanks he gave it to them, saying, 'Drink from it, all of you; for this is *my blood* of the *covenant*, which is poured out for many for the forgiveness of sins'" (Matt 26:27–28, emphasis added)

The rupture of the love relationship of mutual faithfulness between God and his people is overcome and healed by the faithfulness of Jesus in shedding his blood because of his faithfulness to God the Father. Jesus, uniquely among humankind, keeps the covenant, being faithful to God and fulfilling God's hopes. This is a triumph for humanity because Jesus stands as the human representative of the human Israel. By faith in Jesus as Israel's representative, Israel can be faithful to the covenant of love despite her own faithlessness. But, as we noted in passing, Israel, as God's chosen, is herself a representative—of all humanity. By faith in him, we all, whether Jew or gentile, can be represented by the faithful One, in whom we have the hope of the covenant of love.

CONCLUDING NOTE

The rest of the chapters of this book will focus on virtues that the apostle Paul lists in his encouragements to churches in such passages as Gal 5, Eph 4, 1 Cor 13, Phil 2, and Col 3. These virtues are qualities that Christians exhibit in their relating to fellow human beings. They are what I earlier called the Christian "humanistic" virtues, to draw a contrast with the "theological" virtues that we've considered in the present chapter.

Paul mentions, again and again in his letters, the virtues of human relating. His purpose in harping on them is to encourage members of the churches to acquire them or deepen them or persevere in them. However, in commending these qualities, Paul uses a peculiar set of terms that reflect a Christian understanding of the role of Christ in the economy of human holiness and righteousness, and a peculiar understanding of our own activity (what may be called our "agency") in relation to Christ's role. For example, in the Colossians passage, he uses the vocabulary of putting on and taking off clothing, as though the virtues are external items like your shirt and pants. They're not like other attributes, such as your height and hair color that belong wholly to you, but more like clothing that you put on. And we're to "take off" or "put away" the corresponding vices. Similarly, Paul talks about "letting" the peace of Christ rule in your heart. There it is: the shalom of Christ. Now, just submit to it: let it rule in your heart. In Rom 6, he also talks about "yielding" yourself or "submitting" or "putting yourself under" servitude to Christ, as though, in a sense, you're only half an agent or you're the agent of somebody else who's giving the directions. In the same vein, Paul talks about our having been re-created in Jesus Christ for good actions, which God prepared beforehand that we should walk in them (Eph 2:10).

In the chapters that follow, we will seek to understand the Christian virtues of inter-human relations in such Pauline terms. And we will try to make our philosophical explorations in a way that has "pastoral" import: a way that helps us grow in wisdom and all the virtues.

FOR DISCUSSION

1. Why are faith, hope, and love called "theological" virtues? How are the theological virtues related to the virtues that Roberts calls "humanistic"?

2. How are faith, hope, and love similar to the virtues of a married couple?

3. How are faith, hope, and love (and other virtues) like and unlike habits?

4. How does Jesus figure in the faith, hope, and love of Christians?

Chapter 7

GRATEFUL GENEROSITY AND FORGIVINGNESS

A STORY OF GENEROSITY AND INGRATITUDE

You're in a bind. You desperately need some money to pay the rent. If you don't get a loan, you'll be on the street. You go to a friend with your story. You ask for a loan, but Mary *gives* (!!) you the rent money plus some extra for groceries. When you ask, "How can I ever repay you?" she says, "Let's just call it even." You're amazed. And what a relief! You thank Mary profusely. Her gift makes the difference, and you get back on your feet. In a couple of years, you have a comfortable salary at a stable company and are building a savings account, currently at a high rate of interest. Then your friend George comes to you. He's in a bind like the one Mary helped you out of. You've been doing so well, seeing that savings account grow. If you give George what he needs, it's going to mean six months of no growth in savings. You tell George you're very sorry, but you just can't do it right now. He'll need to look elsewhere. When Mary hears about this, she's angry.

She thinks you don't understand about gifts and gratitude. Your failure to understand, she thinks, isn't due to low intellect, but a perverse heart. You're an ungrateful person. She doesn't think about repayment to herself. You took her gift in the wrong spirit, according to the wrong dialectic, the wrong way of thinking. She gave it in the spirit of grace, and you received it in the spirit of advantage.

What is a dialectic? A dialog is a conversation, a talking and thinking back-and-forth between two or more people. You say something and your partner says something *in response*. If your partner says something irrelevant to what you just said, then it's not quite a dialog. What you said and what he said aren't relevant to each other. It's not responsive, just two people saying things, one after another. A "dialectic," as I'll use the word here, is linking thinking, a back-and-forth that makes sense. You might say it's a dialog, not between people, but between ideas, for example, the ideas of generosity and gratitude. The dialectic of gratitude and generosity shapes a way of acting and feeling, a way of understanding life, a coherent moral outlook. Reciprocity integrates these ideas: gratitude is a fitting response to a generous action, and the grateful person responds by thinking generously himself. In fact, his gratitude, if genuine, is itself a generous attitude. A dialectic is an integrated way of making sense of the world or some part of the world. In a sense, a dialectic *is* a world. And genuine gratitude puts us into that world, that way of thinking and feeling and acting.

GRATEFUL GENEROSITY

The dialectic of the gift is a way of thinking and being about goods and people. The two basic moves in this dialectic are giving and receiving, or receiving and giving. To think about goods and people in the dialectic of gift is to think of the goods as gifts and the people as receivers and givers of gifts. To think about goods and people in the dialectic of advantage is to think of goods as advantages and people as ones who can provide you advantages or stand in the way of your advantages (say, by competing for your advantages).

When you go for groceries, you enter a "world" governed, not by the dialectic of gift, but by that of advantage. Here, the back-and-forth is between cost and benefit, and they are held together with the notion of an exchange, a trade or a trade-off. Benefits are advantages and costs are disadvantages. Benefits are gains and costs are losses. If you're a customer, you trade a cost (money) for a benefit (apples); if you're the grocer, you exchange a cost (apples) for a benefit (money). Ideally, you both get what you want: the grocer gets money, you get apples. You try to get the most benefit for the least cost, and the grocer does the same. The difference is just that for you, the benefit is food and the cost is money; for the grocer, the cost is food and the benefit is money. When the grocer who is thinking advantage gives out free samples, he figures the cost of the samples may give him the advantage of selling more groceries, and when the customer tries a sample, she figures its advantage as a free snack or a way to find products that are worth the money.

You can see the similarity between the dialectic of gift and the dialectic of advantage: in both, there's a "transaction": something given and something received. But the ethical and spiritual difference is great. In the dialectic of advantage, each party's goal is to maximize his or her advantage. In the dialectic of gift, each party's goal is to benefit the other party. When I go to buy apples, I just want to get the best and most apples I can for the least money possible. When I give you a gift, if I give it in the spirit (dialectic) of gift-giving, I want *you* to have a benefit, typically at a cost to myself. I'm not looking to indebt you to myself or get any other payment. My advantage (if you want to call it that) is just that you get the advantage.

The dialectic of the gift belongs to the love of the other and the other's love for you. The dialectic of advantage usually belongs to the love of self, though it can be subordinated to the dialectic of gift. For example, in carefully choosing the gift that will please you most, I might think in the dialectic of advantage about how to get the best deal I can (and thus the best gift I can get you) for my money. The question about character is really about which of the two dialectics is basic or dominant in my thinking: What is my *end* goal? If I observe the ethical limits of correct trading, then perhaps I express the virtue of justice. But if my thought is dominated by the notion of gift, then I express the virtue of grateful generosity.

Another relationship between the two dialectics also occurs. Not only can the dialectic of advantage be subordinated to the dialectic of gift. The two can be mixed in such a way that they "temper" one another. If the grocer is a generous, respectful, compassionate person, he won't be as ruthless in his profit-taking as he would be if his thought reflected only the dialectic of advantage. To serve the community, he will be willing, say, to make less profit than he might. He might decline to move his grocery store to a more affluent neighborhood because if he did, the people in his current neighborhood would suffer hardships. In the spirit of generosity, he gives up some advantage, while still trying to make a profit.

The mixture of the two dialectics can also be reversed, so to speak. Gifts can be given, in part, because of the advantages they bring to the giver. Considerations of tit-for-tat can be mixed in with seeking advantage for the other. A rich person might help a poor person, *not only* with the thought that the poor person needs the help, but *also* with the thought that it's safer for people like himself if the poor are not allowed to sink too low. Regardless of the variations in these ways of thinking about exchange, it remains true that they are distinct. This is shown by the fact that there are cases of thinking purely in terms of advantage and thinking purely in terms of gift.

Why is Mary angry? She thinks: I gave you money in the spirit of gift and you took it in the spirit of advantage. You showed this by your unwillingness to give a similar gift (because of the disadvantage to your savings account) when the opportunity came. According to Mary, gratitude is genuine only when it's in "dialog" with generosity. It's a proper recognition of generosity, and in that recognition, it participates in the spirit of generosity. Your gratitude, if it's real, will induce generosity in you, because of the way of thinking it belongs to. If you receive a gift, but don't get into that dialectic by being grateful for it, then you've refused to understand the gift as a *gift*. Instead, you think of it as a "freebie," a lucky windfall in the dialectic of advantage.

In effect, Mary sought to bless you in a deeper way than merely helping you out of a pinch. And she sought that good life for you by thinking about you that way herself. She was inviting you into a happy, generous, really humane way of thinking. Instead of accepting this larger gift, you turned its means into a measly "advantage" for yourself. In your ingratitude, you missed the cue. You didn't join her in this gracious way of thinking, but insisted on living in the bleaker, colder, graceless world of advantage.

PART TWO: SOME CHRISTIAN VIRTUES

BEING RATIONAL

The dialectic of advantage has been called rational. According to this way of thinking, cost-benefit analysis is the essence of practical rationality. Thinking efficiently in cost-benefit terms is all it takes to be rational. And so we get what is called rational choice theory, a theory in economics according to which cost-benefit thinking *is* practical rationality. To call it rationality is to give it status.

What does a Christian say? Cost-benefit deliberation and perception is indeed a *form* of rationality (see Luke 14). But we can ask, "What shall we take to be a benefit?" and "What shall we take to be a cost?" For example, is a gift to another a cost or a benefit to the giver? Cost-benefit analysis can be deployed with a variety of motives. Rational choice theorists talk about "preferences," just as I have talked about "concerns." The concerns are more basic to character than "rational choice," because what you care about determines who you are. You will remember Robbiebud and Donniejohn (ch. 3). Both of them may deploy "rational choice" thinking, but they differ greatly in character—and thus, in their rationality. From a Christian perspective, Donniejohn is the rational one, and Robbiebud, for all the efficiency of his cost-benefit reasoning, is irrational because his preferences are unhealthy for a human being. He takes adulation by others and power over them to be his good and tries to maximize these at minimized cost. But these aren't in fact his good. Even if he is rational in the *form* of the *way* he pursues his good, he is irrational in pursuing a false good. His real good, as a human being, is to belong to an order of generosity and gratitude, an order of peace.

In chapter 3, we looked at Rom 12:1–2, where Paul gathers up all that he has said in the first eleven chapters of the letter about God's generosity to us sinners in Jesus Christ, and proposes that "therefore," let us hand ourselves over in similar generosity to God's service and the service of our fellow creatures. And he describes this generous service to God and fellow creatures using a word (*logikos*) from which we get our word "logical." It *just makes sense* that if we've been treated generously in a very big way by God, then we would take a generous attitude toward life. If God's generosity doesn't have that effect on us, then we haven't understood it. We didn't catch the drift of it. We haven't appreciated its bearing. The "logic" or "rationality" of grateful generosity is reflected in the petition at the end of the Prayer of General Thanksgiving in the Book of Common Prayer:

> And, we beseech Thee, give us that due sense of all Thy mercies, that our hearts may be unfeignedly thankful, and that we show forth Thy praise, not only with our lips, but in our lives, by giving up ourselves to Thy service, and by walking before Thee in holiness and righteousness all our days.[1]

COMPETITIVE ADVANTAGE

What would it be to "walk before God in holiness and righteousness"? Again, it may be instructive, in understanding what is glorious, to place it against the dark background of its contrary in which, sadly, we can dimly see shadows of ourselves.

Competition pits one person or group against another. The winner wins *because* the loser loses and the loser loses *because* the winner wins. To win is to compare advantageously with the one who loses. Even if the winner plays badly, he wins if only the loser plays worse. That's the logic,

1. See http://www.commonprayer.org/offices/gthank.cfm.

the dialectic of competition. It can be playful, but what makes it so (if it is so) is that it's dominated by the dialectic of generosity—the dialectic of advantage isn't ultimate.

The competitive version of the dialectic of advantage, which is opposite the dialectic of generosity and gratitude, is not just a general form of rational thought, like the cost-benefit dialectic, but is what I called, in chapter 3, a moral (in this case, *im*moral) outlook.

Robbiebud's thinking is ruled by the dialectic of advantage, in an ultimately competitive way. Advantage, in his view, is advantage in comparison with others. It is advantage *over* others. To Robbiebud's way of thinking, the good is power over others and their voluntary self-subordination to himself in loyal attention, praise, and adoration. He doesn't love or respect them; their importance is simply to be unimportant in comparison with Robbiebud. That's what a "win" is, in the dialectic of his twisted mind. In contrast, Donniejohn the Christian also follows a dialectic of advantage, but he conceives the good—his own good *together with* the good of others—as an order of peace in which all persons treat each other graciously, caring about others for their own sake and being cared for in the same spirit. In Donniejohn's view, the order of peace is the ultimate advantage. It is glorious, and the people who are fit, by their character, to enjoy and promote it are glorious. To his mind, there are, in the end, no winners or losers among human beings, though some people are unfortunate, and his attitude toward them is compassion and the generous effort to lift them up. In the spirit of advantage, he looks for the most cost-effective way to do so. The dialectic of advantage is in service to the dialectic of gift. In Robbiebud's mind, the dialectic of advantage serves a dialectic of competitive self-importance which we might call the dialectic of envy. The dialectic of the gift rejoices in the other's successes and bemoans the other's troubles, while the dialectic of envy rejoices in the competitor's comparative troubles and bemoans the competitor's comparative successes, since they betoken one's own failure.

Except in special playful contexts, Donniejohn doesn't think of others as competitors. To his way of thinking, it would be a big advantage if his neighbor's pain could be relieved, or if the teenager next door had more self-confidence, or if he and his fellow church members loved God more. And he's inclined to think, in the dialectic of advantage, about how to bring about such goods as these.

THE GOODS WE GIVE

What is one generous *with*? The answer, I think, is "givable goods." Anything that's both good and can be given can be the stuff of generosity. We may associate generosity mostly with "material" goods: money, food, shelter, clothing, tools. We call such things "goods" because they assist people in living a good life. But many goods, and even some of the most important ones, are not "material." Time, energy, attention, the benefit of a doubt where someone seems to have transgressed, encouragement, praise, companionship, a listening ear, advice, compliments, kind words, a sympathetic gesture, forgiveness. The list could go on. All these are goods, and many of them are more primally in the spirit of generosity than material goods. Furthermore, the "nonmaterial" goods are more often, and often more, within our reach than material goods. Material goods can be given grudgingly, or with an indebting burden or a domineering or self-righteous tone—thus, emptied of the spirit and thinking of true generosity. Even though such goods may "help," in a way, the giving doesn't contribute much to an order of peace.

PART TWO: SOME CHRISTIAN VIRTUES

The generous person has an "eye" for goods she can bestow on others. They stand out for her. With an appetite she bespies them lurking in situations, and they look to her like opportunities.

I took two of my grandchildren, Isaiah (seven) and Addie (nine) out for ice cream. Sibling competition between these two often yields an unpleasant exchange. However, to my delight, they're working on it. While we ate, Isaiah told a long story, and as it went on and on, Addie started humming annoyingly in the background, and persisted. I asked her a couple of times to let Isaiah go on, and when I got no results or only brief relief, I spoke to her sharply enough that she stopped and Isaiah completed his story in peace. I asked the two of them what they liked about their church, and they mentioned that the sermons are pretty understandable. Then Isaiah piped up that "Daddy says Addie's sermon notes are even better than his own." Now that was a generous thing to say. Were his mindset the dialectic of envy (as Addie's had been a few moments before), he might have thought of the fact with resentment and kept his mouth shut. But in the mindset of the gift, he opened it gladly, and out came a gift. It was doubly generous: a voluntary gift of encouragement to Addie and a forgiving gesture to boot. It was a good and beneficial thing, within his power to give. And he gave it.

THE GIVER OF GOODS

When we're grateful, it's because we got something good. But we didn't *just* get it. We got it *from somebody*, who *intentionally* gave it to us, and did so for *our own good*. In other words, we are grateful not just *for* something, but *to* somebody, for the gift, yes, but even more importantly for the good will towards us. In still other words, gratitude is paradigmatically a response to acts of generosity: the intentional giving of goods *to us*. We may speak loosely about being grateful for the nice weather for our picnic without thinking that God picked this weather just for our picnic. But that isn't a standard case of gratitude, and we might as well have said that we are "glad" about the weather being so nice.

I would imagine that Addie was encouraged by what Isaiah said about her sermon note-taking. It built her up. She gladly accepted it and (I hope) it impressed her with Isaiah's good will toward her. Potentially, it deepened slightly her bond with him. And (I also hope), it eroded her tendency to annoy him and strengthened her tendency to be generous with him. I further hope it weakened his tendency to annoy her. If all this is true, it was a contribution to the order of peace. All this will depend on their adopting the dialectic of gift into their philosophy and vision of life. If Addie simply thinks, "Oh, points for me. People see how special I am with my note-taking," without being grateful *to* Isaiah for his generous remark, then it won't have these beneficial effects on her character.

Great-minded persons, according to Aristotle, are generous (liberal, *eleutheros*), but they don't like being in the position of the grateful person, which they regard as inferior (*NE* 4.3). People with "great" souls don't want to be indebted to others. So, if they do happen to receive from another's generosity, they don't like to admit it. The fact that we (both Christians and non-Christians) tend to think of such an attitude as small-minded suggests how different our idea of human greatness is from Aristotle's. Consider Mark 9:33–36, where the disciples were thinking in the dialectic of envy and Jesus taught them to think, instead, in the dialectic of gift.

Here is an exercise in learning generosity. Change envy (an especially nasty exercise in the dialectic of advantage) into generosity. How? When you feel envy of someone, praise her to her face or others' face for whatever you're inclined to be envious of. So you turn envy into admiration. Envy is stingy, admiration generous. You switch sides: you trade an against stance for a pro stance. You ally yourself with your "enemy" and so lose an enemy and gain a friend and make a little contribution to an order of peace.

FORGIVINGNESS

When someone has wronged us, we speak of "getting even." (To account for our tendency to go overboard, we might say, "*At least* even.") It's as though the offender and his action put me down and I want to restore myself to his level (or higher). Revenge looks like a variant of the dialectic of advantage, perhaps even in its competitive version, the dialectic of envy. My wrongdoer has put me down, and I'm competing with him for the prize of top dog.

When you're angry at someone who has wronged you, you see yourself as disadvantaged in a transaction or exchange. In stealing some of your property, or revealing something embarrassing about you, the wrongdoer has put you down, either neglecting your dignity or directly despising you (as vermin, you don't have any dignity). Forgiveness is a willingness to absorb the disadvantage created by being wronged, to forswear anger, to adopt an attitude of being even, when you are disadvantaged by a wrong. Without condoning the wrong or getting revenge, you say (as it were), "Let's call it even." You eat the unevenness (even if it tastes pretty bad). You don't count the offender's debt against him or her.

Christian forgiveness expresses a concern for the order of peace, the kingdom of God. In this, it is rooted as much in a concern for the offender and your relationship with him or her and for the wider social order as it is for your own comfort. In this it differs from what we might call "therapeutic" forgiveness, whose sole or main purpose is to rid yourself of the burden and adversity and personal suffering of anger and hatred. Dr. Phil refers to this non-Christian kind of "forgiveness" when he says, "Forgiveness is not about another person who has transgressed against you; it is about you. . . . It is a gift to yourself, and it frees you. . . . Do it for yourself."[2]

By contrast, Christian forgiveness is a kind of generosity, and to be a forgiving person is to be generous. Forgiveness is a gift that you bestow on the one who has hurt you. And it's a response to God's generosity: "God proves his love for us in that while we still were sinners Christ died for us" (Rom 5:8). "Bear with one another" says Paul, "and, if anyone has a complaint against another, forgive each other; just as the Lord has forgiven you, so you also must forgive" (Col 3:13).

Generosity gratefully received generates a bestowing generosity.

FOR DISCUSSION

1. What is a "dialectic"? Compare the dialectic of gift with the dialectic of advantage.

2. Is Roberts right that your gratitude is genuine only if it makes you generous? What is it about generosity and gratitude that links them in this tight way?

---

2. McGraw, "Ten Life Laws," law 9.

3. What is the dialectic of envy, and how does the dialectic of gift rule it out?
4. How is forgivingness a kind of generosity?

Chapter 8

COURAGE, SELF-CONTROL, AND PATIENCE

COURAGE

IN PURSUIT OF HIS mission of love, Jesus deliberately "set his face" (Luke 9:51) toward Jerusalem, knowing he would be tortured and killed there. The disciples were warned not to preach about Jesus, but obeyed God rather than the human authorities—and got beaten up for it (Acts 5:17–42). Stephen the disciple addressed a crowd with truths they didn't want to hear—and was stoned to death (Acts 7:54—8:1). Paul tells of his many encounters with dangers and violence and threats of death as he announced far abroad the good news of Jesus (2 Cor 6:4–5, 8–10). And yet he steadily persisted. Many who might start on some such venture as these would, when faced with threats like this, quail and give it up.

PART TWO: SOME CHRISTIAN VIRTUES

The classical Greek word for courage (*andreia*, manliness) doesn't occur in the New Testament (though a related verb occurs once: 1 Cor 16:13). But stories of courage dot its pages. The courage of early church members has contributed, in ways beyond our ability to calculate, to the blessings of the gospel that you and I enjoy in the church today. They loved us, so to speak, though they didn't know us. It is a mark of courage as a virtue that it serves as support for other virtues, in particular, the virtues of caring. The early Christians were moved to their acts of courage by devotion—to God, to the Lord Jesus, to their fellow believers, and to humanity. We will see that this is true also of such Christian virtues as self-control, perseverance, and patience. They serve as auxiliaries to the main Christian virtues of love (faith, hope, compassion, generosity, forgivingness, and so forth) when those virtues meet impulses that rise in the human heart to resist the pursuit of good: fear, anger, discouragement, distaste, impatience, sensory appetites. And the strategies by which Christians address these psychological adversities often exploit the virtues of caring that the adversities threaten.

Motivation by the virtues of love makes courage and acts of courage distinctively Christian. Courage is always moved by some concern or other. But the concern doesn't have to be love. Like the heroes in Homer's *Iliad*, you might act courageously for the sake of your honor. A business owner might make a courageous investment for the sake of her business. You might courageously enter a house in flames to rescue a cherished painting. We might even think the concern could be evil: to kill three thousand people and destroy a magnificent building, it took courage for the 9/11 terrorists to sacrifice their lives in a plane crash. This is why I think courage is not, in itself, a fully moral virtue. The motive for a courageous action may be morally admirable, or it may not be. And whether it is depends on whether it's moved by a virtuous concern. Unlike the virtues of caring, courage isn't defined by what moves the courageous person to act, but rather by the obstacle it overcomes: threat and fear. Analogously, the virtue of patience manages impulses of impatience, while self-control manages episodes of appetite (sex, food, drink) and emotions (for example, anger, contempt, and envy).

BOLDNESS

An attitude related to courage—boldness or confidence (*parrhēsia*)—is mentioned many times in the New Testament, and in biblical thinking seems to have the status of a Christian virtue, though Paul doesn't mention it in any of his lists. It is associated with speaking on behalf of God's kingdom, and also with approaching God personally. Like courage, it's an ability to manage or circumvent fear. We might think of it as a Christian courage that specializes in speaking for God and approaching him.

Acts 4 reports that Peter and John, by the power of Jesus, healed a well-known man who was lame from birth. In the astonishment and commotion that followed this public healing, they captured the attention of the people. Peter used the occasion to proclaim the resurrection and lordship of Jesus. This speech annoyed the priests, the captain of the temple, and the Sadducees, and they arrested Peter and John and jailed them overnight. When the officials questioned them the next day, they again preached the message about Jesus. The officials were amazed at the boldness of Peter and John, who were uneducated. Nobody would have expected this.

With the people all around and the formerly lame man standing there looking chipper, the officials felt their hands were tied, so they just ordered Peter and John not to say anything else about Jesus. Again with boldness, the apostles responded that they were going to talk about Jesus anyway, because God required it. The officials must have been rather taken aback by this answer, but they couldn't do much, so they threatened them again and sent them on their way. The apostles returned to their Christian companions and told them what had happened. The church responded with joy and prayed, "And now, Lord, look at their threats and grant your servants to speak your word with all boldness" (Acts 4:29). This prayer shows us three things: the church regarded boldness as a good trait (a virtue); they thought it was from God (a fruit of God's Spirit in us); and were aware that Christians can be scared into timidity (and so need to be prayed for).

The apostle John, in his First Letter, stresses a rather different context for the virtue of boldness: the judgment of God. He points out that if we love God and one another, we won't be afraid to be in God's presence (see also Eph 3:12). We'll be confident (bold) before God. Why? In connection with fear and love and the "final" judgment, we tend to think that it's about whether our love will be judged adequate. We think: if my love is perfect, I'll pass the test with flying colors. I'll have nothing to fear from the judge.

I don't think that's what John has in mind. In fact, if that's the right way to think about the matter, we ought all to be trembling in our boots: the final judgment is a terrifying prospect for all of us. After all, John's the one who says that if we think we're without sin, we deceive ourselves (1 John 1:8). Here's what he says about boldness:

> And now, little children, abide in him, so that when he is revealed we may have confidence [boldness] and not be put to shame before him at his coming. . . . Little children, let us love, not in

word or speech, but in truth and action. And by this we will know that we are from the truth and will reassure our hearts before him whenever our hearts condemn us; for God is greater than our hearts, and he knows everything. Beloved, if our hearts do not condemn us, we have boldness before God; and we receive from him whatever we ask, because we obey his commandments and do what pleases him. . . . God is love, and those who abide in love abide in God, and God abides in them. Love has been perfected among us in this: that we may have boldness on the day of judgment, because as he is, so are we in this world. There is no fear in love, but perfect love casts out fear; for fear has to do with punishment, and whoever fears has not reached perfection in love. (1 John 2:28; 3:18–22; 4:16–18)

I think John's thought is that love by its nature excludes fear. To love something is to see and appreciate its goodness, while to fear something is to see and feel its potential harming aspect. It's not that I evaluate my love for God and neighbor and judge it to be fully up to snuff, and then conclude that I have nothing to fear from the test. Rather, love casts out fear because we're so glad that God is there and he is so attractive, so lovable, so glorious, that his very goodness casts out fear. The greater the love, the more it's about the beloved and the beloved's splendid and stupendous wonderfulness. Love casts out fear because it swallows self-concern. The more perfect our love, the less we're thinking about ourselves and the more we're filled with wonder at the beloved's splendor. We are lovers: God is love, and as he is, so are we in this world as we abide in him. That self-forgetfulness, that rapt attention to what is surpassingly wonderful, makes us bold. It dissolves our defenses and makes us "hungry" for the beloved.

Again, we see that this virtue of (our) strength depends on another virtue, a virtue of caring—in this case, love—about something that isn't us. The apostles speak the word of the Lord "with all boldness" because they love the Lord and his word, and they greet the Lord in his judgment with the same boldness for the same reason.

VIRTUES OF SELF-APPLIED STRENGTH

Yet, courage and boldness belong to a group of virtues that I call *enkratic*. The word that both Aristotle and the apostle Paul use for self-control is *enkrateia*, which is a Greek word for strength. The virtues of caring are all modes of caring, especially caring for people: in their suffering (compassion), in their having wronged you (forgivingness), in their vulnerability (gentleness), and so forth. Courage and other enkratic virtues are defined, not by what we care about, but by the obstacle they overcome. They are powers of self-management, especially in resistance to "temptations"—impulses that go contrary to virtue or good sense or our more considered goals. Courage is strength against fear; self-control is strength against inappropriate appetites, inertias, and emotions; perseverance is strength against discouragement, fatigue, and boredom; patience is strength against impulses of impatience.

These emotions, impulses, inertias, and appetites are subjective states. But in each case, we may think objectively instead of subjectively: with courage we face *danger*, with patience we put up with *people*, with forgiveness we forgive *offenses* and *offenders*, with self-control we resist *racism* and *gluttony*, and so forth. But in each case, we need to resist the object only because of our impulsive response to it. Without the impulse's responsiveness to the object, the object has no power to pull us off course. This is why the enkratic virtues are variants of *self*-management. Ultimately, we work on our impulses, not the objects that provoke them.

As abilities, powers, or strengths, the enkratic virtues involve know-how. The courageous person knows how to handle her fear; the persevering person knows how to overcome impulses to quit; the self-controlled person knows how to manage her anger and her appetites for food and drink and sex; and so forth. Some of these know-hows are fine-grained intuitive psychological skills comparable to the fine finger– or lip control of a musician playing an instrument. (We "play" the enkratic virtues on ourselves.) If asked, "How do you do it?" the person with courage or self-control might be at a loss to answer, except in the grossest terms. Other aspects are strategic and much easier to talk about: say, avoid situations where sensory temptations are likely to arise. That, too, is self-control.

In the last section I quoted John as saying that perfect love casts out fear. This is a formula for the how-to of the enkratic virtue of boldness. The ability in question is knowing how to manage our fears about speaking God's word and facing God's judgment. How do we manage them? What is Christian boldness as an "ability"? Taking our cue from John's thinking, the answer must be that we try to keep our attention on God's goodness: the glory of Christ, his coming to us, his dwelling among us, his love for us especially as expressed in his voluntary death, and his resurrection from the dead. I think that if we are filled with a sense of that goodness, and so love it and him, then our boldness will follow. In the church's preaching and liturgy, it provides "the means of grace" for our use in the practice of boldness.

We need boldness because we have fears and anxieties. As an ability that is a different virtue from the love it exploits and serves, boldness is skillful self-management. It's a readiness to remind ourselves of God's radiant goodness in the light of which our little fears are fading shadows.

SELF-CONTROL

I've named the present group of Christian virtues (the "enkratic") after self-control because all are abilities to manage impulses in ourselves that need to be managed if our love for God and one another is to be free and fully expressed. "Self-control" is, in a way, a catchall term for these virtues.

Nevertheless, we do use "self-control" especially in connection with certain kinds of impulses. If you're fasting and you feel an urge to grab a cookie, you'll call on your self-control to resist. If a beautiful woman you're talking with is dressed provocatively, you'll exercise self-control in keeping resolute eye contact with her. If you're having a somewhat boring conversation with one who needs your ear and you hear a more interesting conversation across the room, you'll apply your self-control to keep your attention fixed on the one who needs it and to shut out the more interesting one. If you're giving testimony in a trial and the opposition lawyer tries to provoke you to anger, you may need self-control to keep your cool. If you're with "important" people and feel the urge to call their attention to your impressive accomplishment, and you practice humility by suppressing the urge, the power you call on is self-control.

PATIENCE AND FORBEARANCE

Love is patient, says the apostle Paul. It doesn't insist on its own way (1 Cor 13:4–5). We who are stronger ought to bear the weaknesses of those who are less strong. We shouldn't be about pleasing ourselves, but about pleasing our neighbors to build them up in goodness (see Rom 15:1–2). Paul talks here about a couple of special "applications" of love. They are ways you love others when they "try" you. Perhaps they are quarrelsome, or often late for appointments, or remiss in showing you respect in other ways. Perhaps they insist on *their* own way. It's "natural" to be annoyed and impatient with such people. We think about *our* time that gets wasted; *our* projects that get delayed or hindered, the disrespect to *ourselves* that such nitpicking indicates. The situation devolves into a struggle of ego against ego. Our interactions become an unpleasant conflict with resentment on both sides, even if we preserve a civilized appearance. And the resentment grows with rumination. We chew and chew on our grievances, savoring the bitterness of unfairness and slights both real and imagined. If pleasing our neighbors builds them up in goodness, our impatience tears them down, and us with them in a downward spiral.

Understandably, psychotherapy and the self-help literature related to therapy make us think about ourselves. If I go to a therapist or the self-help shelf, it's because *I* have a problem, some deficiency or trouble in my life that I hope to get help with. Furthermore, and for a similar reason, the enkratic virtues require us to think about ourselves. One aspect of virtue ethics is a kind of therapy. The purpose of virtue ethics, and of Christian virtue ethics in particular, is to improve our understanding of excellent human character traits, and this study applies most importantly to your and my own growth in virtues. We can't do that without thinking about ourselves. But there are two very different ways to think about myself, and the dynamic I just described contains them both. Let's call them the loving and the unloving ways.

The unloving way is inclined to be impatient with others who bear unpleasantly or inconveniently on our interests. In practicing it, I "insist on my own way": I give priority to myself and my agenda. I insist on my "rights." "Self-care" trumps other-care. I'm afraid that psychotherapy and self-help often tend toward this unhealthy and unchristian way of thinking about ourselves. We noted in the last chapter how Dr. Phil changes forgiveness as a kind of love into a device for purging yourself of unpleasant and destructive emotions. (You have a "right" not to be burdened with anger at someone who's wronged you. "Do it [forgive] for yourself!") The self here is a sovereign individual who can and should insist on his or her own "rights," not so much a member of a greater community that she serves and from which she gratefully receives. The therapeutic mentality doesn't produce egoism out of nothing: it simply confirms and enhances the natural human tendency toward selfishness. So psychotherapy and self-help sometimes boost the dynamic downward spiral and relational troubles that I mentioned.

We have seen that courage and self-control, as self-management skills, can be put to work in the service of other ends than Christian peace and love. Patience is an ability to stay on an even keel despite irritations: irritations associated with waiting, with uncooperative washing machines and complicated word-processing programs, with students who are disinclined to study. Patience in these contexts can serve many purposes: food production, the drying of paint, clean clothes, efficiency in typing, and the turning out of competent young people. There's nothing especially Christian about patience in itself. It is the service of love—for the neighbor, for the church, for the world—that turns patience into a Christian virtue.

DEVICES OF INTEGRITY

The enkratic virtues are oppositional: they oppose or control fear, impatience, resentment, anger, untimely appetites, impulses of laziness, discouragement, bad habits, and so forth. They do so, ideally, in the interest of the good, and thus of loving what is good: the neighbor's flourishing, obedience to God. For example, a Christian uses self-control to be faithful to her spouse, patience to practice compassion for those who are suffering, and boldness to speaking God's word. So it is part of the practice of these enkratic virtues not just to oppose bad impulses, but to encourage good ones: affection for your spouse, distress at the sufferer's distress, and eagerness to speak on God's behalf. But if those good impulses were completely spontaneous and free of opposition from contrary forces, we wouldn't need to practice self-control, patience, or boldness.

The liability posed by those contrary impulses is not just the inconvenience of obstacles like hills that need to be climbed and brush that needs to be cleared. They are often expressions of what Paul calls "the flesh" (Gal 5:19–21): impulses flatly contrary to Christian identity.

Who are we—we Christians? We are people who love God and his kingdom, devotees of Jesus, and so we are people who love our neighbors. That's our identity. Earlier in this chapter we heard John say that God is love, and as God is, so are we (Christians) in this world (1 John 4:17). If that's so, then some of the forces that enkratic virtues resist threaten our very identity: when we give in to our fears, our lusts, our impulses of vengeance, our envy and greed, we aren't being ourselves. We're compromising our identity and letting ourselves be ruled by an occupying foreign power. We're giving in to forces of personal disintegration. This, I think, is why Robert Adams calls the enkratic virtues "structural."[1] The structural aspects of a building—the foundation, the framing, the outer walls—enable it to resist wind blowing against it and the movement of the earth under it. They provide its integrity, its ability to remain an integral building rather than a pile of broken materials that were once a building, such as we see in the aftermath of a tornado or an earthquake. Wind and the movement of the earth threaten to pull the building apart. In a similar way, our fears, our lusts, our impulses of vengeance, our envy and greed threaten to disintegrate us as lovers of God and our neighbors. The enkratic virtues are a defense that's within our powers, with God's help and the resources of our faith.

FOR DISCUSSION

1. How are courage, self-control, and patience related to virtues like compassion and generosity?

2. How is boldness a Christian virtue, and what is it good for?

3. What do we do to ourselves when we act with courage or patience or self-control?

4. What kind of difference makes the difference between one enkratic virtue and another (say, between patience and courage, or self-control and perseverance)?

---

1. Adams, *Theory of Virtue*.

Chapter 9

COMPASSION, GENTLENESS, AND KINDNESS

Let's return, now, to some virtues of caring. I've noted that the virtues of caring for fellow human beings have the form of generosity. They are traits of character by which we are prone to care about *other* people's interests, pleasures, protection, well-being, reconciliation, vulnerabilities, and relief from suffering, and care about these for *their* sake. In chapter 3 we talked about moral outlooks, and said they are conceptual frameworks—ways of thinking—that enable and dispose us to "see" things from a moral perspective. The virtues of caring belong to a way of thinking about self, recipient, gift, and exchange that I have called the dialectic of the gift. This pattern of thinking stands in contrast with the dialectic of advantage, which is also a way of thinking about ("seeing," experiencing, feeling) yourself, others, what you "exchange," and the nature of "exchanges." To have any of these virtues—generosity, gratitude, forgivingness, compassion, gentleness, kindness, truthfulness, justice, loyalty—is to be disposed to think (about life—self, others, and goods "exchanged") in the dialectic of the gift. Even the love of justice, which may seem to be an exception since justice is giving people what is their *due*, is the generous love of a device for maximizing the well-being of others and minimizing harm to them. A love of "justice" that considers only your own advantage as it is served by the rules of justice is not the virtue of justice.

COMPASSION

Compassionate people are prone to think of others' well-being, as our perception of their suffering calls our attention to the issue. Compassion is a specialization of generosity. It's generosity towards sufferers. It is repeatedly illustrated in Jesus's emotion and action toward sufferers, as well as in his parables.

In the town of Nain, when the Lord saw a widow following the bier of her recently dead son, he had compassion for her and told her, "Don't weep." Then he came forward and touched the bier, and the bearers stood still. And he said, "Young man, I say to you, rise!" The dead man sat up and began to speak, and Jesus gave him to his mother (Luke 7:11–15). Two blind men called out to Jesus as he walked by. Moved with compassion, Jesus touched their eyes, and they could see (Matt 20:29–34). Jesus came ashore from the lake and saw a great crowd with some sick people: "He had compassion for them and cured their sick" (Matt 14:13–14). He called his disciples and said, "I have compassion for the crowd, because they've been with me now for three days and have nothing to eat; I don't want to send them away hungry, lest they faint on the way" (see Matt 15:32). "As he went ashore, he saw a great crowd; and he had compassion for them, because they were like sheep without a shepherd; and he began to teach them many things" (Mark 6:34). (Note that ignorance can be a kind of suffering or deficiency, and teaching an act of compassion.) A leper came to him begging him, and kneeling, said to him, "If you choose, you can make me clean." Moved with compassion, Jesus stretched out his hand and touched him, and said to him, "I do choose. Be made clean!" (Mark 1:40–41). Stories of forgiveness are also typically stories of compassion, given that the guilt that is relieved by forgiveness is a burden.

Also, in his parables Jesus depicts good people as moved by compassion. For example, a wayward son, having messed up his life and wasted his inheritance, set off and went to his father, intending to humble himself and ask for a menial job on the farm. But while he was still far off, his father saw him—bedraggled, dirty, exhausted, discouraged, in rags, and burdened with guilt—and was filled with compassion; he ran and put his arms around him and kissed him (Luke 15:20). A traveling Samaritan came by a wounded man in the ditch; and when he saw him lying there bloody, bruised, and moaning, he was moved with compassion, and went out of his way to help him (Luke 10:33). A servant owed his master far more than he could pay from even a lifetime of work, and out of compassion for him, the lord of that slave released him and forgave him the debt (Matt 18:27).

In each case, the person for whom Jesus or his parabolic character feels compassion is in some kind of trouble, distress, or deficiency. He is attuned to their distress because he cares about them as fellow human beings. He sees it. He notices it. It stands out for him. Compare this perceptiveness with the moral blindness of the rich man in the parable in Luke 16. Lazarus lay at the rich man's gate with sores that the dogs came to lick. And the rich man walked by Lazarus daily and hardly noticed, or if he did notice, it was with annoyance that this disgusting scene was playing out at *his gate*. By contrast, when Jesus sees the sufferers, he feels their distress as a compelling reason to help them out, because he sees them as fellow human beings. Compassion is all about the *other* person, yet the other person's suffering calls on *me* for action. Without compassion, I just note that the other is suffering and go on my way. With compassion, by contrast, I have a "stake" in the other's well-being that I become aware of by seeing that the other is suffering.

What is the nature of this stake, this motivational pressure on *me* to relieve the *other* of his suffering? Philosophers sometimes explain it by speaking about my desire for relief from *my* discomfort[1] or the motivating consideration of *my* happiness.[2] This kind of explanation has some plausibility, because the emotion of compassion is uncomfortable, and the compassionate person does typically feel some relief on seeing the sufferer relieved. The other's suffering or deficiency distresses the compassionate person. But it can also distress us for reasons other than compassion.

The screams of a sufferer can grate on your nerves. The sight of wounds can make you queasy. You can find funerals distasteful because meeting someone in mourning depresses you. The question is: How does the distress of *compassion* move us? I'm proposing that we feel uncomfortable because we care about the other's well-being, and we see that the other is suffering. The emotion of compassion is a feeling of frustration of our concern for the other's well-being. It's true that we desire to escape the distress, but *as compassionate*, we want to escape it in a very particular way: by the other's restoration to peace. To escape it by taking a drug or by hiding the other's distress from ourselves doesn't satisfy the compassionate concern.

---

1. Greenspan, *Emotions & Reasons*.
2. Nussbaum, *Upheavals of Thought*.

Jesus is our model of compassion as a virtue. He is concerned about the *other's* well-being—the widow at Nain, the blind men by the road, the sick people in the crowd and the friends and relatives who brought them along, the hungry crowd, the hapless crowd, the suffering leper. Jesus no doubt felt distress at their distress and relief when their distress was relieved. But if his thinking is "their well-being is part of my well-being, so let me help them," it seems that this extraneous thought about himself spoils the compassion just a bit. Jesus's own distress and his relief are secondary and incidental by-products of his concern for the sufferers' well-being, not the considerations in view of which he relieves their distress. The compassionate person cares about the other, and when he sees that other in distress or deficiency, he desires to relieve or lessen it. Compassion has the form of generosity.

GENTLENESS

Let's say that gentleness is anticipatory compassion with a special reference to our own potential for harming others. It's an alertness to, and tendency to shun what, in our own actions, might cause hurt. Like all the variants of *agapē* (generosity), gentleness is a caring about the well-being of other people. Like compassion, it's a negative concern: an avoidance of or repugnance for harm, in this case prospective harm of others caused by oneself. If you're gentle, you're careful, in your speech and actions, not to hurt others. You adopt this stance out of love for them.

The Greek word that I'm translating "gentle" (*praüs*) has sometimes been translated "meek." For example, the King James Version of Matt 5:5 is "Blessed are the meek: for they shall inherit the earth." And in Matt 11:29 the KJV has Jesus saying, "I am meek and lowly in heart." Meekness, as it is understood in contemporary English, is the contrary of boldness or confidence, which we saw in the last chapter to be a Christian virtue. Meekness is a shrinking timidity or shyness. It isn't a Christian virtue. The apostles (at their best) and Jesus were not meek, but bold and confident. Nevertheless, Jesus was gentle, and the apostles strove to be so. The gentle person, in taking care to minimize provocation and hurt in what she does and says, may act with boldness and confidence. Presumably, the gentle will inherit the earth because they love, hope for, and promote by their gentleness, the order of peace to which God has destined the earth in Christ. When the kingdom comes, the gentle will fit right in. Jesus invites us to put on *his* yoke and learn from *him*, because he is gentle and humble of heart (Matt 11:29). In this way, our souls will find rest, because gentleness and humility tend to sow peace where they are practiced.

Gentleness is a special way of loving the neighbor. It's in the same spirit as forgivingness, generosity, and forbearance. It's a fruit of the Holy Spirit (Gal 5:23). Being gentle is part of what it takes to live a life "worthy of the calling to which [Christians] have been called" (Eph 4:1–3). That is a calling to harmonious community with all people, to reconciliation where such community has been disrupted, and an order of well-being (peace).

Gentleness contrasts with being harsh or inconsiderate of the feelings of persons. As such, it's associated with practical wisdom—in particular, with what we might call circumspection: moral awareness of the context, including the consequences, of one's action. The apostle James speaks of "gentleness born of wisdom" (Jas 3:13). The gentle person wisely anticipates how his words or other actions may affect the people he's interacting with. And if they seem to him likely to provoke a quarrel or to alienate those people or to escalate tensions, he will seek to evade or soften them in a way that avoids such results. But the gentle person is also truthful and just, and so will, in seeking to avoid provocation, seek also to say what is true and promote what he takes to be justice. You can see how being properly gentle takes wisdom.

To the churches of Galatia Paul says, "My friends, if anyone is detected in a transgression, you who have received the Spirit should restore such a one in a spirit of gentleness" (6:1). By the wisdom of life in the Spirit of God, the more mature members of a congregation work to restore to fellowship someone who has transgressed. Perhaps he sinned against members of the congregation, creating tensions and alienation. This work of restoration is to be carried on in a spirit of sensitivity to and avoidance, where possible, of what may provoke any party to further rancor and alienation. Gentleness is the recommended style of demeanor of those who seek reconciliation and restoration of peace.

A related context for gentleness is debate. When the issues of a debate seem momentous to the debating parties, the interpersonal dynamics can become bitter. People can take intellectual criticism as personal attack (and sometimes it truly becomes that). Among immature people, even disagreements about trivial matters can become occasions for anger and rising impulses of petulant revenge. In his Second Letter to Timothy, Paul says that "the Lord's servant mustn't be contentious, but kind to all, instructive, tolerant, gently correcting critics so that God may convert them to a knowledge of the truth" (2 Tim 2:24). Since Paul depicts the Lord's servant as here talking to a non-Christian, the likelihood of disagreement is high. The servant wants to convince the other of a truth that the other is resisting, perhaps vigorously. Here, the Lord's servant will likely implement gentleness by careful word choice, by humble phrasing, by questions in preference to direct challenges, expressions of agreement where possible, and by bodily cues: friendly tone of voice, smiling eye contact, full and charitable attention to what the other is saying. Gentleness communicates respect.

Like the other traits we're discussing in this book, gentleness is a quality of character or personality. It's more like a personal policy or habit, an ingrained and regular quality, than a particular type of action. As with all the virtues of caring, it's a way of thinking about life and relationships. Actions are gentle to the extent that they express or display or imitate this quality of the person. We can learn to *be* gentle people by *acting* gentle, and by thinking in gentle terms: "How can I avoid making this person fearful or angry or ashamed or envious?" Compassion should be practiced gently, because it irritates some people to be "pitied." Gift-giving should be practiced gently because some people feel uncomfortable being "indebted."

We could distinguish between having a practice ("It's my practice to . . .") and actually practicing the practice. The person whose practice is to be gentle will not practice gentleness in everything he does, any more than a person who practices law practices law in everything she does. There's a time to practice law and a time to practice motherhood or sky-diving. "It's my practice to be gentle" doesn't imply "*Here* I will practice gentleness." If I'm wise, then whether I practice gentleness "here" will depend on the situation of the "here." A brave soldier may choose, in his wisdom, to retreat or hide, yet without ceasing to be a brave man.

Some situations may not call for gentle action. A person with the virtue of gentleness may sometimes judge that a situation calls for her to be harsh. The wise person may discern that a situation calls for harsh action. Jesus is gentle, but we see that he doesn't always act gently. When he cleanses the temple with a makeshift whip, driving out cattle and money changers (John 2:13–22), he isn't practicing gentleness. When he pronounces woes on the cities that wouldn't listen to his announcement of the kingdom of peace (Matt 11:20–24), he isn't practicing gentleness. "Be angry," says Paul ("but don't sin") (Eph 4:26). When Jesus calls the Pharisees hypocrites and white-washed tombs (Matt 23:27–28), he seems to have chosen to be harsh. Presumably, in his wisdom Jesus saw these situations as calling for harsh, rather than gentle, action. Harsh actions don't *exemplify* gentleness, but they're compatible with being gentle. Sky-diving actions don't exemplify the practice of law either. But they're compatible with being a practitioner of law.

KINDNESS

Kindness emerges in a person who lives under the sway of the Holy Spirit of Christ (Gal 5:22). It is one of those qualities in which we Christians should daily clothe ourselves (Col 3:12) as we seek to honor Jesus. Paul says, "Love is kind" (1 Cor 13:4). The word that's often translated "kind" (*chrēstos*—not to be confused with *christos*: Christ, the anointed) isn't very specific. In that way, it's a bit like "good." In fact, "good" is one of the words that is used to translate *chrēstos*. So many things can be good in so many different ways! That leaves us room to fill in the kind of goodness that is intended in each context. God is good (*chrēstos*—Luke 6:35); old wine is good (*chrēstos*—Luke 5:39); and love is good (*chrēstos*—1 Cor 13:4). The kind of goodness varies from context to context and we discern the kind by our sensitivity to context.

But also, words have "resonances" from context to context. When someone says, "The old [wine] is very good [*chrēstos*]," she means to say it's mellow (it doesn't "bite") and it tastes good. It goes down smoothly; it's a pleasure to swallow. Perhaps we should keep that in mind when we hear that love is kind (*chrēstos*): it too goes down smoothly and tastes good. People tend to like it when they're offered some. We who are Christians, notes Peter, have turned our backs on all the forms of interpersonal bitterness, because we have tasted that the Lord is *chrēstos* (1 Pet 2:3). If we've been in close fellowship with him for a while, his kindness has rubbed off on us, and others will tend to feel it.

In Matt 11:30, Jesus says that his yoke is *chrēstos*, and the NRSV translates, "My yoke is easy." The yoke fits comfortably. Just as the old wine doesn't "bite," the yoke doesn't pinch or chafe the shoulders on which it rests. It's comfortable. Love, being kind, also doesn't pinch or bite the loved one: it *feels* good, and that not-pinching, not-biting, that fitting comfortably and feeling good and going down easy, is intended by the one who loves. The kind person knows love's power and has become good at conveying to others the comfort and good feeling of being loved. That's part of the Christian's good will towards the one loved. And in her kindness, the Christian is indiscriminate: just as our Father is kind to the ungrateful and the wicked, so we should be merciful to everybody (Luke 6:35–36), whether or not they're kind to us. In being kind even to the unkind we mirror the character of God.

A contrast may throw light on the virtue of kindness. We talk about "nice" people and people being "nice." The word "nice" is nice, because it's so nicely bland and empty. "Nice" has all the adaptability of "kind," but without the integrity and depth of the Christian concept. Christian kindness isn't just being nice. People can be nice for many different reasons, but if they don't have love, they aren't kind, no matter how nice they are.

Let's return for a moment to Donniejohn and Robbiebud, from chapter 3. Both men are nice to people sometimes, but Robbiebud's niceness isn't kind, because it's conditional, selective, and changeable. In chapter 3 we talked about differences in outlook, and we saw the difference between Donniejohn's character and Robbiebud's to be largely a matter of how they "see" the world—a difference in their patterns of thinking and caring about life and especially human relationships. As Robbiebud sees life, people are to serve him in one way or another. That's what he cares about, and that's why he's nice, when he's nice. When he thinks a person may serve his ends, he's nice to her. Maybe he wants her to give him money, or he wants to sell her a Bible or an NFT. Maybe he wants her to vote for him—or have sex with him. And when she becomes an obstacle to his ends, he becomes indifferent or gets angry and vengeful, and isn't nice at all. If Donniejohn is nice, it may well be out of kindness, the Christian virtue. He cares about *you*, *your* well-being, *your* comfort and improvement, *your* having a place in the order of peace. If you're grumpy or opposed to him in some way, he may be nice to you anyway, because he's kind and sees your humanity through the disguise of your grumpiness and opposition. He's not trying to get anything from you, or to use you for any purpose. He knows God's love and naturally wants to pass it on to you. This is how he sees you and what he wants from and for you.

CONCLUSION

Compassion, gentleness, and kindness are variants of love. They are occasional "ways" of loving your neighbor. They are dimensions or departments of the enterprise of Christ's kingdom. Each belongs to a context or occasion that arises from the nature of the human creatures to whom we direct our love: compassion to their suffering, gentleness to their vulnerability, and kindness to the receptiveness of their humanity.

FOR DISCUSSION

1. How does the distress of compassion move the compassionate person to help the sufferer? Do you agree with Roberts's answer? What is the relation between compassion as a virtue and compassion as a kind of emotion?

2. What is gentleness? How are gentleness and wisdom related to one another? Can a person who is gentle ever act harshly? If so, how is this possible?

3. How does being kind differ from being nice?

Chapter 10

TRUTHFULNESS, JUSTICE, AND LOYALTY

THE VIRTUES DISCUSSED IN this chapter, like those of chapters 6, 7, and 9, are virtues of caring. They are ways of loving God and your neighbor. But, unlike those other virtues, these are *indirectly* about God and neighbor. More directly, they are concerns about devices of love. The truthful person loves truth, the just person loves justice, and the loyal person honors specially defined individuals or entities. Justice as love of neighbor is concern that the principle be met that *all get what is due them*. Loyalty is love of neighbor as mediated by some special relation, such as *my child* or *my spouse*, *my parents*, *my friend*, or *my country*. And truthfulness is love of neighbor by respecting reality and representations of it. But the wise and mature Christian understands that honoring truth, justice, family arrangements, and friendship bears on the good: the kingdom of God. It bears on peace: on the love of God and the happiness and well-being of God's creatures. And the mature Christian's *understanding* of these things is an aspect of her mind that contributes to the status of truthfulness, justice, and loyalty as Christian personal excellences. This understanding of her dispositions helps to make *her* a hearty participant in God's enterprise.

TRUTHFULNESS

What is truth? Let's say that truth is reality. It's what is, what was, what will be, and what is eternal. But if so, why call it *truth*? Why not just call it reality? When we call reality truth, we evoke the specter of falsehood, in particular, the idea of a representation of reality—a belief, a claim, a hypothesis, a statement, an ideal, an image, or a model, for example—that may or may not be true *of* the reality that it's about. Truth is reality, all right, but reality thought of as possibly represented, and so also as possibly *mis*represented. Reality is truth ("the truth"), and representations that match it are true. A sentence is true if what it says matches what it's about. "Lincoln was the sixteenth president of the USA" is true if and only if Lincoln was the sixteenth president of the USA. A gem that appears to be a diamond is true if it's a diamond. A friend is a true friend if she lives up to the ideal (or a certain threshold of the ideal) of a friend.

We connect with reality by representations of it. We look, and our eyes "tell" us this and that. We investigate and get information. People tell us things. We listen to the news. We read. In all such cases, we use representations to get in "touch" with reality.

Connecting with reality is important to us in various ways. If I ask, Where are my keys? and the answer I get is true, I am more likely to find my keys than if the answer is false. If the "news" I read and believe is fake, I may vote for a presidential candidate who will serve himself rather than my country. Our work goes better if we know the relevant truths. We relate better to others if we have accurate information about them and if, when they tell us things, they tell us the truth.

So truth is practically important in a variety of ways as a means to many valuable things in our daily life. Even the most inveterate liar will probably want to know the truth that he's lying about. If he goes beyond this and starts believing his own lies, losing contact with reality (truth), his mind and his "world" will become incoherent. He'll be practically incompetent, even in his own perverse terms.

Truth is important to us also in itself. Aristotle points out that it's in our nature to want to know the truth, quite apart from any practical use the knowledge may afford (see the opening paragraph of his *Metaphysics*). You can't know something unless it's true. You can believe something that isn't true, but then your belief doesn't count as knowledge. You can *think* you know something when you don't; but you can't actually know it unless what you believe is true. In wanting to know, we are wanting contact with the truth.

We naturally care about truth, both because of how it serves our practices, and in itself. But truthfulness as a virtue includes caring about the truth as it bears on others, and especially as *we* have some role in causing others to believe things. We have some control over whether others have this indispensable commodity of contact with reality.

To deceive another is to reduce that person's competence and to deprive him, in some measure, of a basic good in life (namely, contact with reality). We may have good reasons for limiting or reducing his competence, in case he is bent on using it to do harm. So withholding truths from some people in some circumstances, and even deceiving them, making them positively believe what is false, *can* be the right thing to do. But many of our lies and deceptions and lack of candor are motivated by selfish protection of our interests or fear of embarrassment. In many of these cases, it would be more loving to tell the truth as we see it. Enhancing people's competence and appreciation of truth when we can is usually the generous thing to do, and often it's an obligation.

Truthful people are careful to avoid leading others to believe what isn't true. Because we care about the good of others, we want others to have the use of truth as well as the intrinsic good of contact with reality, and to avoid the inconvenience and even outright evil of believing what is false.

In the fourth chapter of Ephesians, Paul lays great stress on dangerous deceptions, ones that are especially destructive because of the importance of Christ as an object of knowledge and the place of this knowledge in building up Christ's dwelling place on earth. False beliefs about Christ and ourselves in relation to him can stymie the proper growth and unity of the church, and thus the maturity of humankind, which is properly to be found in the church.

If Christ is who he and the church say he is, the question of truth in this case is momentous, both practically and intrinsically, and the case can function as a sort of paradigm for the virtue. Like other virtues of caring, it is a disposition of the heart. Truthfulness is caring appreciation of the importance of truth.

So truthful people are ones who love truth for its own sake and for its power to enhance their competence. And, because they love their neighbors, they love the truth of representations for the sake of their neighbors. They want their neighbors to share in this good.

Paul commends "speaking the truth in love" (Eph 4:15). The context might be that of telling difficult and painful truths, and Paul would be instructing us that when we must tell hard truths we should do so gently and with kindness. But equally, the context might be seeing the power of truth-telling in the practice of love—that telling the truth is itself an important benefit (an act of love) to the one who receives it.

The virtue of truthfulness bears not only on the conveyer of representations, but also on the receiver of them. In Gal 4:15-17, Paul addresses such a case. Some of the Galatians seem to have taken his truth-telling as an act of enmity against themselves. We don't always like the truth. Some of us don't like being corrected. We like the comfort of supposing that we're already in possession of the truth, so that when it is suggested that what we take to be truth isn't truth, and that some other thing is, we resist, and, like these Galatians, react with hostility to the truth-teller. Truthful people will be on the lookout for truths, even the uncomfortable ones. Because they love truth, they are "good listeners" and tend to be willing to consider seriously what others say. But, also because they love truth, they use a plausibility filter that quickly dismisses known inveterate liars and people who obviously don't know what they're talking about.

To be a truthful person is to be one who cares about or respects reality, especially in connection with representations of it. It's in our human nature to care about reality in these ways, and it's a perversion or an immaturity for us not to care and thus not to be careful about truth—about reality and the truth about reality.

JUSTICE

In the Bible, *dikaiosynē* is usually translated "righteousness" rather than "justice," as it usually is in translations of other Greek writings, such as Plato and Aristotle. This difference

PART TWO: SOME CHRISTIAN VIRTUES

in translation reflects that biblical righteousness is broader than what we usually call justice. It isn't just giving people the good things or punishments that are due them by right, or desert, or status. The righteous person, in biblical terms, is the person of trusting faith, of devotion to God. She is the generous person, the forgiving person, the gentle and kind and compassionate person. All of part 2 of this book is about *dikaiosynē* (righteousness) in this broad sense. Biblical "justice" is overall moral excellence. As such, it includes what we, more narrowly, call justice: honoring people's rights, respecting their property, paying our bills, not cheating, administering the law evenhandedly.

In this section, I will speak of the virtue of justice in this narrower sense. To be a just person is to be someone who cares deeply that people—all people—be treated justly: that they be given what is due them, that their rights be respected, that they be treated equally before the law, and so forth. It's a lively readiness to notice and recognize justice and injustice wherever they occur. By extension, it's caring about laws and institutions: that laws be framed so that people get what is due them, and that institutions be arranged in ways that promote people getting what is due them. The virtue of justice is a "sense" of justice: both an emotional sensitivity to justice and injustice—a joy in one and grief at the other—and a sharpness of mind about what actually is just and what isn't.

Rabbi Shai Held notes that rabbinic commentators tried to discern what it was about the character of Abraham and Moses that prompted God to choose them for their special and central roles in representing God among humanity. A prominent answer was Abraham's and Moses's sense of justice.

In one rabbinic retelling of Abraham's call, he looks at the world and sees that it's "in flames"—the innocent suffer, the powerful oppress the weak, the guilty escape punishment and live luxuriously on their ill-gotten gains, and so on. Abraham wonders: "Is anybody in control here? This world isn't up to standard." The energy of Abraham's concern for justice squeezes this urgent question out of him. The answer comes back in God's voice: "I am the owner of the world." It's a confirmation of Abraham's uncompromising sense of justice, an assurance that justice will ultimately prevail, and a call to collaborate to that end.

Genesis 18:16–33 illustrates Abraham's independence of mind about justice. The Sodomites were terribly depraved, and the Lord was inclined to level the city with fire and brimstone. But then he thought he'd better share his plan with Abraham, since he had chosen him as a moral expert to "charge his children and his household after him to keep the way of the LORD by doing righteousness and justice" (Gen 18:19). So he consulted with Abraham. Right away, Abraham saw that leveling the city might involve a lot of innocent people in Sodom losing their lives along with the sinners. This wasn't fair, so he bargained with God: "If you find fifty innocents in Sodom, would you reconsider?"—"OK." "What about forty-five?"—"Well, all right." And he went on chiseling (in a very gentle, humble, and respectful way) until he got the Lord down to ten.

Rabbi Held points out that Moses was a worthy successor of Abraham as a leader who cared that all people be treated fairly.

> As soon as Moses grows up, the book of Exodus tells us, he immediately intervenes in three scenes of interpersonal brutality. Witnessing an Egyptian taskmaster beating an Israelite slave, Moses steps in and kills the abuser; seeing two Israelite men scuffling, he tries to separate them and admonishes the offender. Having been

forced to flee Egypt, Moses arrives in Midian and observes a group of male shepherds mistreating young Midianite women at a well; without hesitating, he drives the shepherds off and waters the women's flocks (Exodus 2:11–17).[1]

Spontaneously, Moses finds injustice intolerable. Injustice distresses him and he strikes on behalf of justice, seemingly with little deliberation (though I suppose that previously, he had done a lot of thinking about justice and understood it well). This spontaneity is the emotional character of a just person. Again, it's a mark of justice that it doesn't matter who the parties are: "Moses stands up for an Israelite against an Egyptian oppressor, for an Israelite against a fellow Israelite, and for a Midianite against other Midianites (and for women against men)."[2] Also, it's noteworthy that in none of these stories is Moses himself a recipient of the justice in question: his concern is about other people receiving justice.

Little children easily talk about what's "fair," and about being treated equally. But only at a later stage of development do we really care about other people being treated equally, and only at a still later stage, at which few of us arrive, do we care about all other people being treated equally. A love of "justice" that considers only or primarily our own advantage or the advantage of our group as it is served by the rules of justice isn't the virtue of justice. Also, the impulse to "punish" those who "deserve" it, to "get back" at those who have hurt us, is natural and primitive. Little children have it or develop it early. This disposition appeals to a primitive concept of justice, but not to the one that governs the virtue of justice. The virtue of justice is an interest in an infinitely disinterested principle.

1. Held, *Judaism Is about Love*, 61.
2. Held, *Judaism Is about Love*, 61.

LOYALTY

If justice is for everybody, loyalty is to a special few. I can be loyal only to what I think of as in some sense belonging to me. For example, I'm loyal to this particular person because he's my son. I'm loyal to this other because she's my wife or my friend. I'm loyal to this ball team because it's in some sense "my" team. I'm loyal to this country because it's my country. Like friendship, loyalty requires character but it isn't merely a matter of character. It's a relation to another. There's no such thing as loyalty full stop. I can't be loyal without some particular other person or entity to be loyal to, "defined" as "mine." Loyalty is a bond between two, felt and practiced by at least one of the two.

Three of the Ten Commandments (Exod 20) enjoin virtuous loyalties: (1) You shall have no other gods before me, (5) honor your parents, and (9) refrain from adultery. Thus, loyalty to God, loyalty to parents, and loyalty to spouse—*your* God, *your* parents, and *your* spouse.

To be loyal to this person or entity, I must think of him or it as potentially depending on me in some way. Where this dependence emerges, I show my loyalty by supporting her or it. The practical implication of my loyalty to a friend, for example, or my country is that I support my friend or country. I do things on its behalf, especially when it's under stress or threat, and when it depends on me or others like me. To be loyal is to be trustworthy to give support.

The bond of loyalty is tested and contested by competing appeals. For various reasons, it may be difficult to support the object of my loyalty when he or it stands in special need of support. I may have to sacrifice time that I would otherwise devote to some important or enjoyable activity. I may have to choose among the demands of competing loyalties. In loyalty to my wife, I may have to resist the attractions of other persons, cutting off relations with them that

I enjoy or that are important to me in other ways. In vocal support of the object of my loyalty, I may put important relationships at risk. I may even put my life at risk, say, in showing my loyalty to my country.

It might seem odd that loyalty to God, as the first commandment calls for it, presupposes that God depends on me for my support. Isn't God too independent to need support? But we noted in chapter 6 that faith, which is a kind of loyalty, is a response to a covenant or agreement (a deal) between God and his people. By making a covenant with Israel God opens the possibility that Israel might not keep its part of the deal. Thus, people who keep the commandments, who adore God and love their neighbors, are in fact supporting God in loyalty to him.

To be the recipient of someone's loyalty is to rely on, to trust, the loyal one to support and to refrain from undermining (more generally, to be attentive to and careful of) your well-being. The obverse of loyalty is trust. The wife of a loyal husband counts on him not to betray her with another lover and to "be there for" her in the daily circumstances of life. The parents of loyal children count on their children to support them in times of trouble, as do children of loyal parents. Loyalty doesn't strictly entail the counterpart attitude of trust on the part of the counterpart person. (Some counterparts aren't persons. You can be loyal to a country or its constitution.) Where there is both loyalty and trust, there is, to that extent, peace—the good. That is why our tradition commends various loyalties.

Though the seventh commandment is framed negatively and behaviorally—*don't commit adultery*—Jesus teaches us to read it as having attitudinal import (Matt 5:27–28) and as a variant of *you shall love your neighbor* (Matt 7:12; 22:40; see also Gal 5:14). Jesus seems to imply that loyalty to someone is a matter of attitude, and not just behavior. What kind of attitude? Let's say you refrain from lusting, not out of respect for your spouse, but because you think it will give you annoying dreams and lower the quality of your sleep. Otherwise, you'd find it fun to fantasize, and you'd be fine with it. This wouldn't be a very good example of loyalty *to your spouse*. So, following Jesus, it might be legitimate to formulate the commandment in positive and attitudinal terms. The seventh commandment would be "You shall love your spouse with special devotion." That would be full-blooded loyalty to a spouse. The command to be loyal to parents is already couched in positive and attitudinal terms: we are to honor them.

So far, we have spoken only of virtuous loyalties. These three are virtuous because they make for an order of peace and well-being.

When Donald Trump pressed James Comey, then director of the FBI, for his loyalty, he was asking Comey to be reliable in supporting him. He was asking, can I trust you to support *me*? He was asking for Comey's loyalty, not to the constitution or the country, but to Trump personally. Knowing Trump as we now do, he was saying, as it were, I want to be able to count on you to lie for me when my agenda requires it; to stop investigations of criminal behavior when I or my associates perpetrate those crimes or when those investigations would interfere with my purposes. I want to be able to count on you to prosecute my enemies without regard to legal and moral justifications. I want you to concoct narratives that support my interests, whether or not they're true. All of this is what your loyalty to me would imply.

Comey replied, mentioning his own truthfulness, "I was not 'reliable' in the way politicians use that word, but [Trump] could always count on me to tell him the truth."[3]

3. Quoted in Taylor, "Comey," para. 6.

Comey saw, I suppose, that the vicious loyalty for which Trump was asking was inconsistent with an order of peace. He also saw, no doubt, that loyalty to a vicious man requires vice—in this particular case, mendacity and injustice. As a man in pursuit of virtue, Comey was repelled by the prospect of such an ugly loyalty.

CONCLUSION

Truthfulness and justice are virtues. They are indirect ways of loving our neighbor. Loving truth, we love our neighbor by sharing it with him or her. Loving justice, we aspire to and promote a social order in which every human being gets what is due him or her. Loyalties, by contrast, are not always virtuous, though ones that are properly directed serve, like truthfulness and justice, the order of peace that is the kingdom of God.

FOR DISCUSSION

1. What is truth, and why is it important? What attitude does the truthful person take toward truth?

2. How are the virtues of truthfulness, justice, and loyalty ways of loving God and people?

3. How do just and loyal people, in their different ways, contribute to the order of peace?

4. How can loyalties be vicious, and what does this imply about the virtuousness of virtuous loyalties?

Chapter 11

JOY, WISDOM, AND HUMILITY

IN THIS FINAL CHAPTER we consider three more virtues that play prominent roles in the Gospels and the New Testament Letters. In their different ways, these three saturate the character of the well-formed Christian. Christian joy is an expression of any of the virtues of caring when the concern that is basic to each is satisfied. In this way it incorporates and expresses Christian wisdom: an understanding of our life in the light of the works of Jesus and their coming glorious fulfillment. To understand your "world" in these terms is to rejoice in your life, the life of the church, and the life of the world. Finally, by sidelining the human love of self-importance, the virtue of humility protects those concerns and their corresponding understanding against a tendency that so often threatens to pollute, confuse, and divert them.

PART TWO: SOME CHRISTIAN VIRTUES

JOYFUL WISDOM

Paul includes joy as a fruit of the Holy Spirit (Gal 5:22) alongside patience, kindness, generosity, loyalty, gentleness, and self-control. These last six all seem to be traits of Christian character, and in this book we've been treating them as such. Is Paul suggesting that joy too is a Christian character trait, a virtue? In that case, joy is a formation of character, a personal quality. This is odd. We don't usually think of joy as a character trait. Instead, we think of it as an emotion that we feel at some moments and not at others. By contrast, to have the *virtue* of joy would be to be a joyful *person*. Such a person isn't necessarily *feeling* joy at this moment or that. Rather, he's the *kind of person* who is *prone* to feel (a certain kind of) joy.

Joy always feels good, but it isn't necessarily a good thing. When Judas Iscariot consulted with the chief priests and the elders how to hand Jesus over to them so they might murder him, "they rejoiced and agreed to give him money" (Luke 22:5). They experienced a delicious delight at Judas's betrayal of the Lord. To rejoice at evil is to endorse it, to approve of it, to like it. And to be the kind of person who likes what is evil is to *be* evil—just as, to love what is good is to *be* good. The chief priests and elders felt an evil emotion at the moment when Judas showed his interest in helping them get rid of Jesus. And by doing so, they showed that their hearts were evilly disposed. Mark tells us that Pilate realized that they were prompted by envy (*phthonos*) (Mark 15:10). Envy is a disposition to rejoice at your rival's adversity—in this case, to rejoice at the demise of Jesus because he seemed to them to be a successful rival. The chief priests and elders enjoyed having power over the people, and they saw Jesus as threatening their self-importance. So envious people, it turns out, are joyful people—people disposed to feel joy (under certain circumstances). And their disposition is a vice, a corruption of the human spirit.

Obviously, envy isn't the kind of disposition to joy that Paul identifies as a fruit of the Holy Spirit. That's why, a couple of paragraphs ago, I said that the *virtue* of joy is a proneness to feel a *certain kind of joy*, and more recently said that the vice of envy is a disposition to feel joy *under certain circumstances*. What kind of joy is a Christian virtue? Under what circumstances does the Christian, as a Christian, feel joy?

Paul says that love "doesn't rejoice at evil [unrighteousness], but rejoices together at the truth" (1 Cor 13:6, my translation). The verb Paul uses for "rejoices" (*synchairein*) adds a "with" or "together with" (*syn-*) to the rejoicing. Who are the participants in this rejoicing: *"together with" whom*? And further: since he says that love rejoices not at unrighteousness, we might expect him to say that it rejoices at what is righteous and good; but he says it rejoices at the truth. Why?

To answer the second question first, I think "the truth" is another way of saying "righteousness." But to call moral uprightness "truth" is to connect it in a special way with knowledge, as we saw in the last chapter. Truth is reality as possibly represented (in belief, perception, or claim—but also as exemplified in a person's character: true human being, one who represents humanity as it was intended to be; an exemplar). The virtues make a person a true human being; and the kingdom of peace is the human order for which the virtues fit a person to live a true human life. Knowledge of the truth in this application is the virtue of wisdom. The wise person embodies a true representation both in the sense that he knows what true humanity is and in the sense that he himself is a true human being: he exemplifies the human truth in his character.

Here I think we have our answer to the question about the "together" or the "with." The wise person beholds and understands the good, but she does so only because she participates in it. She works for the kingdom of peace. She embodies the kingdom of peace in her projects and intentions. She's not a disinterested spectator, a "scientist" or "scholar" of the good: she *is* good, and understands the good in large part *by way of being* good and contributing to it. To use language oddly, you might say that the wise person understands with the good; or more naturally, she has an understanding with the good. She and the good are intimate; the two of them have a "relationship." They're of one mind. They're in love.

What does this have to do with rejoicing? Paul notes the possibility of people rejoicing in what is not true, not wise, not good. He doesn't deny that people who rejoice in evil experience real joy. A vengeful person takes real pleasure in getting revenge on his "enemy." A domineering person really enjoys bossing people around; an envious person may take intense pleasure in putting down her rival. These are real joys, but not the kind that fulfills our nature. In fact, the more "real" they are, the more they degrade and corrupt us (see Mark 7).

You might say they are joys, but they aren't happiness. The life of a man who is full of envy, revenge, vanity, and domination may contain lots of joy, if such evil passions are often satisfied in his life. Yet such a man, for all his joys, is not a happy man: he's a miserable specimen of a human being. He isn't disposed to rejoice with the truth, but in what is alien to him and false to the nature of things, if God is the owner of the world. When, in the prayer book's prayer of confession, we say, "Have mercy upon us, miserable offenders," we're not necessarily saying that we *feel* miserable: only that we *are* miserable. To rejoice with the truth is to participate in it; it is to be true yourself—a true human being.

In rejoicing at the past and future coming of Christ, at the relief of suffering, at the forgiveness of sins, at the spread of the gospel, at the beauty of God's commandments, at displays of virtue, at the happy fellowship of the church, at scenes of peace among human beings, at the correction of injustices, and at anything else that betokens the kingdom of God, you are rejoicing at the truth of the world, the world as God intends it to be, a reality that matches God's will. And your rejoicing in this is your own participation in it: in rejoicing at the truth, you're being a true human being: you yourself are "true," part of the truth, a part of that peace and that kingdom. You are in friendly conversation, a kind of partnership, with the good. You're not in opposition, but in harmony, with it. Maybe this is what Paul means to convey with his odd expression "rejoice with the truth."

Why is it important that Christian wisdom be joyful? Wisdom, as an accurate representation of the truth of human nature and the moral nature of the universe, gets classified as an "intellectual" virtue. It's a kind of knowing, a "cognitive" disposition, a disposition to be in contact with reality. It's a disposition of a *mind* to be in contact with *the moral truth*. I've said that joy is wisdom in the sense that it's right thinking and right caring about what is good. It makes *sense* to take pleasure in what is good (and to be put off by what is bad). Wisdom is a kind of moral or spiritual attunement to the good.

Imagine this. A pregnant woman needs a caesarean section to save both her own life and the life of her baby. She is driven to the hospital in an ambulance and has the surgery. The husband arrives a little later and is greeted by an enormously relieved doctor: his wife is fine and he's the father of an eight-pound, healthy daughter! He reacts with indifference to the news and notes, with some irritation, that he was interrupted in the middle of a poker game that he was winning! Let's assume that he understands the facts: the life of his wife and daughter were in danger, and now both are doing very well. He has a new daughter. Still, there seems to be something he doesn't get. If he did understand, thinks the doctor, he would be greatly relieved, joyful, and grateful to all who had a hand in this rescue. But no: he's indifferent, and seemingly more concerned about his ruined poker game.

What does the father fail to understand? I think he fails to understand the *goodness* of the news he's received. It seems he doesn't care about the life of his wife and daughter. At least at this moment, he seems to love his poker game more than he loves them. If this is right, he fails to understand because he fails to feel joy at the good news, and he fails to feel joy at the good news because he doesn't care enough about it. Joy at what is good is a crucial element in understanding what is good. It's the part of the state of mind in which the *goodness* of a good situation is perceived.

We sometimes *contrast* knowing with feeling. The highest quality knowing, we think, is "disinterested," "objective," "not emotional." It's true that when we believe something just because we wish it were true, we distort and degrade our knowledge. Lamentably, this happens all the time. But knowledge and interest aren't separable: What would be the point of knowledge that we're not interested in? And knowledge of good and evil specifically requires that our minds be emotionally engaged, as our illustration of the indifferent husband and father suggests. To understand fully that something is good, we must have some kind of joy about it (relief, gratitude, hope, and so forth); to understand fully that something is bad requires feeling some distress about it (regret, disappointment, sadness, guilt, and so forth). And surely, whatever wisdom is, it's in the direction of *full* understanding of what's good and bad.

The virtues that I've called the virtues of caring—generosity, gratitude, forgivingness, compassion, gentleness, kindness, truthfulness, justice, loyalty—all involve an understanding of what's good and bad. Generosity requires understanding what is good for people and that people are worth being generous with. To be grateful, you have to understand that someone with a good attitude toward you has given you something of worth. You can't forgive without understanding that injustice and revenge are bad and reconciliation is good; and, again, that people are worth being reconciled with. You can't be truthful without appreciating the value of truth and the harmfulness of deceit and the value of people as the ones to whom the truth is to be communicated. And so forth.

The Christian gospel—the "good news" about Jesus and his kingdom of peace—throws its special light on all these good and bad things. In its light we now understand better how the good is good and the bad is bad. The understanding of all this is Christian wisdom, a wisdom that centers on Jesus and his order of peace. The messengers who announce to the shepherds (Luke 2:10–11) the arrival of the savior explicitly describe the message as joyful and glorious: "And the messenger said to them, 'Don't be scared. Because, look! I bring you a message of great joy which is for everybody, that today a rescuer is born for you in the city of David, which is Christ the Lord'" (Luke 2:10–11). Then more of the heavenly messengers show up, saying, "'Glory in the highest to God and on earth peace among people of good will'" (v. 14, my translation)

Christianity is a joyful way of thinking about human life. Yes, it throws light on dismal evil; indeed, it makes evil look even more clearly and darkly evil than it looks to the naked eye. But it does so by accentuating the positive: by giving us reasons for hope, gratitude, admiration, relief, triumph, and pride. All these emotions are variants of delight. The Christian virtue of joy is a disposition—an ingrained habit—of thinking about our life in the terms of the gospel of Jesus. The gospel gives us reasons for joy—for hope, gratitude, admiration, relief, triumph, and pride. In these emotions we manifest our Christian wisdom.

HUMILITY

Humility is neither a virtue of caring nor an enkratic virtue, though it interacts crucially with both kinds of virtues. I propose that humility is a purity of heart—specifically, purity from the moral pollution of what we might call "self-importance." We human beings have a tendency to rivalries with one another for "status," for power, for attention, for privileges and honors. We desire comparative superiority of various kinds, but our aim in all of them is self-importance.

Our desire for self-importance isn't just the desire to be important. The desire to be important—to be "somebody" in the eyes of our loved ones, our friends, and God, to accomplish something worth being remembered for—is healthy and fully compatible with the virtues of caring. To care about our importance as persons, and to feel satisfied that we do have that kind of importance, is a virtue that we might call "proper pride."

Self-importance, by contrast, is comparative and competitive: to care about self-importance is to want to be *more* prominent, to have *more* privileges, *more* power, *higher* status, to be *more* the center of attention, than certain others whom we regard as rivals. To be conceited is to take satisfaction, not just in our excellence, but in other people's being less excellent than we are. To be pleased in our arrogance is to take satisfaction in having greater privileges and entitlements than our rivals, and to be satisfied in our vanity is to think of ourselves as more admired and applauded than our rivals. There is a zero-sum symmetry about self-importance: the more important you are, the less important am I; the less important you are, the more important I am, where you and I are rivals. You can see, I think, that self-importance is incompatible with the spirit of generosity and the love of neighbor. In this dialectic, a neighbor is a rival: somebody to "keep up with" or (which is even better) to stay ahead of. If you can't keep up with her or get ahead of her, you start to resent her and she takes on the shades of an enemy.

To the extent that you succeed in achieving self-importance, you do so by making some others less important—by demeaning them, at least in your own mind and the minds of a few like-minded others. Our vocabulary of vice gives names to several specific devices of self-importance: arrogance (being more privileged and entitled than others), vanity (being more the center of approving attention than certain others), domination (having more power than others over others), snobbery (being a member of some in-group that excludes "lesser" persons). We might think of envy as a paradigm of the vices of pride (self-importance). Another paradigm is conceit, being conceited. You might say that conceit is what envy aims at; but envy is most evident in the bitterness of failure to have achieved conceit.

A person with the virtue of humility is someone with a very low level of arrogance, vanity, domination, envy, grandiosity, or any other such vice of pride. Perfect humility, which probably doesn't occur among ordinary sinful human beings, would be a complete absence of interest in self-importance and therefore a total lack of arrogance, vanity, self-righteousness, domination, hyper-autonomy, envy, conceit, grandiosity, and any other vice that's a device for self-importance.

Let's illustrate the virtue of humility with two biblical examples. The first is John the Baptist (John 3:25–30). Some of his disciples came to him, apparently worried that John, who had been drawing big crowds, was being supplanted by another, even more popular rabbi named Jesus. John reminds them that he himself isn't the Messiah, and that his role has been to introduce the Messiah. He compares the situation to a wedding, at which the bridegroom is properly the center of attention. The "best man," by comparison, is at the bridegroom's service. When he hears that the groom has arrived and the wedding can begin, he "rejoices greatly." Applying this pattern to himself and Jesus, John says, "For this reason my joy has been fulfilled. He must increase, but I must decrease" (John 3:29–30).

The vice of pride that is conspicuously missing from John is either vanity or domination. People who enjoy lots of attention because it makes them feel important will be reluctant to forfeit the limelight, letting somebody else be the center of attention instead. Thus, vanity might discourage John from allowing the proper transfer of attention from himself to Jesus. Or, if he doesn't stand in its way, he might at least be sad about having to give up the limelight. Instead, John "rejoices greatly" at the transfer of attention and comments that his joy is now "full." He shows a remarkable lack of a vanity that might dampen his enthusiasm for the inauguration of the kingdom of peace.

Or John's impeding vice might have been domination: the love of power over others as a device of self-importance. By his speech and person, John had had the power to gather crowds to hear him and to be baptized by him. If he had a domineering bone in him, his magnetism must have been self-exhilarating, and this exhilaration of self-importance would have been hard to give up with Jesus emerging on the scene to displace him. His domination would have been an impurity in his love of the kingdom and an impediment to the work he was called to. Instead, John seems to be completely free of it in both senses of the word "free": free *from* moral pollution and free *to* cede his power to another, as appropriate.

Jesus's parable of the Pharisee and the tax collector (Luke 18:9–14) will be our second illustration. Here, the vice of self-righteousness is the kind of pride whose absence would be humility. The scene is the temple. Both men are there to pray. The Pharisee's prayer is explicit about the role of comparison and rivalry in his thinking about his importance: "God, I thank you that I am not like other people: thieves, rogues, adulterers, or even like this tax collector. I fast twice a week; I give a tenth of all my income." The tax collector makes no comparison, let alone any that is advantageous to himself. He simply beats his breast and prays, "God be merciful to me a sinner." This is a penitential prayer. Humility is sometimes confused with penitence, I think because penitence requires humility. But they aren't the same. This is shown by the fact that Jesus is our model of humility, but he's never depicted as penitent. And the humility of John that we just considered has nothing to do with penitence.

If the Pharisee were humble in thanking God for his virtues (and I see nothing amiss about doing that), he would simply thank God for this grace and leave other people's faults out. In verse 9, Luke comments that Jesus "told this parable to some who trusted in themselves that they were righteous and regarded others with contempt." The vice of self-righteousness is not just thinking that you are righteous. If we can acquire anything in the way of virtues, it makes sense to thank God for them. And we can't very well do that without noticing that we have some virtues! No: the vice of self-righteousness requires that in noticing our own virtues, we take invidious pleasure in comparing ourselves with others who are less virtuous than we are. That is one of the vices that the person of humility lacks.

CONCLUSION

Joy, wisdom, and humility are three Christian virtues that penetrate into all the corners of Christian character. Wisdom is our understanding of the whole of our life in the light of Christ and his kingdom of peace. Joy is the disposition to recognize the goodness of what we see by Christian wisdom; and so wisdom can't do without joy. And humility is our protection of that wisdom and joy against the insidious, love-destroying pollution of our rivalrous concern for self-importance.

FOR DISCUSSION

1. If joy can be evil, how can "joy" be the name of a virtue?

2. When is joy required for understanding? Why is it required in such cases?

3. If humility is a "purity of heart," what pollution is it purity from? Why is it important that the person with Christian virtues have this purity?

Postscript

CHRISTIAN VIRTUE ETHICS

ANCIENT THINKERS THOUGHT THAT philosophy, as a love of wisdom, ought to make the whole practitioner into a better specimen of humanity, one who comes closer to fulfilling our human potential. After all, we tend to take on the qualities of what we love. We dwell on what we love and want to spend our time in its presence. And if it's a good thing, like wisdom (which is both beautiful and true), the goodness rubs off on us. How do we get into the presence of wisdom? By thinking its thoughts. As we do this, those thoughts become the second nature of our minds, the form of our souls, the character of our understanding of ourselves and our world.

To the purpose of making us more completely human, the part of philosophy called ethics was central in ancient philosophy. It focused on the moral contours of a mind and that mind's place among the fellow minds with whom it lives. Ethics was about the proper formation of our desires, our emotions, and our understanding of how to live a human life. In a word, ethics was a study of human virtues. It was "virtue ethics," though as far as I know, nobody called it that.

In the second half of the twentieth century emerged another "virtue ethics," this time one that didn't particularly aim at the formation of people, but rather at devising a new way to shore up the foundations of ethics (see ch. 5). Those foundations were still suspected of being shaky after the proposals of the Kantians, the utilitarians, the sentimentalists, and the social contract theorists. Here, virtue ethics was more a project in conceptual engineering than in therapeutic moral psychology. It was mostly for seminar discussions, for philosophy professors and their young captives, rather than for the building up of souls.

Christians have a natural affinity with the ancient style of virtue ethics. The moral cultivation of the community seeking the kingdom of God is a central activity of the church. Philosophy should be a welcome and useful resource in building up the church and its individual members.

In this book, I've suggested that the human good is two kinds of things, or one thing with two sides. On one hand, it's the social order of peace: in our Christian conception, the kingdom of God; on the other, it's the healthy order of the human heart, the form of fitness of human minds to conduct and enjoy that order of peace: it's the virtues: in our Christian conception, the Christian virtues. Wisdom is about the good in these two dimensions. It's a loving understanding of the good. And philosophy is a love of wisdom. So, on the principle that to love the love of x is to love x, philosophy is a love of the human good. In particular, it's an inquisitive way of loving the good, a love by inquiry. To the extent that philosophy succeeds in understanding the good, it is also a love of both the order of peace and the fitness of souls to inhabit and promote that order.

The heart of virtue ethics, as a branch of philosophy, is loving attention to the virtues, and the purpose of attention to the virtues is *virtues*: yours and mine. I think that if we pay attention to them—thinking about them carefully, distinguishing them from one another and discerning how they interact with each other, with emotions, desires, attention, and perception—we'll become more sensitive to their natural call as they speak to whatever virtue is already in us. By the practice of philosophy, we'll be drawn to a deeper, better formation, a truer humanity.

AFTERWORD

IN RECENT YEARS I have written more extensively and more deeply about some of the topics covered in the present introductory survey.

Roberts, Robert C. *Attention to Virtues: An Affective Grammar* Cambridge: Cambridge University Press, forthcoming [2024?].
———. "Gratitude, Friendship, and Mutuality: Reflections on Three Characters in *Bleak House*." In *The Moral Psychology of Gratitude*, edited by Robert Roberts and Daniel Telech, 317–37. Moral Psychology of the Emotions. Lanham, MD: Rowman and Littlefield, 2019.
———. "Joy and the Nature of Emotion." *Journal of Positive Psychology* 15 (2019) 30–32. doi: 10.1080/17439760.2019.1685576.
———. "Joys: A Brief Moral and Christian Geography." *Faith and Philosophy* 36 (2019) 195–222. doi: 10.5840/faithphil2019430120.
———. *Recovering Christian Character: The Psychological Wisdom of Søren Kierkegaard*. Grand Rapids: Eerdmans, 2021.
———. "Varieties of Virtue Ethics." In *Varieties of Virtue Ethics*, edited by David Carr et al., 17–34. London: Palgrave Macmillan, 2017.
———. "The Virtue of Piety." In *Spirituality and the Good Life: Philosophical Approaches*, edited by David McPherson, 47–62. Cambridge: Cambridge University Press, 2017.
Roberts, Robert C., and W. Scott Cleveland. "Humility from a Philosophical Point of View." In *Handbook of Humility: Theory, Research, and Applications*, edited by Everett L. Worthington et al., 33–46. London: Routledge, 2016.

Roberts, Robert C., and Ryan West. "Jesus and the Virtues of Pride." In *The Moral Psychology of Pride*, edited by J. Adam Carter and Emma C. Gordon, 99–121. Moral Psychology of the Emotions. Lanham, MD: Rowman and Littlefield, 2017.

———. "Virtues of Willpower and Self-Possession." In *Endurance*, edited by Nathan King. Oxford: Oxford University Press, forthcoming.

Roberts, Robert C., and W. Jay Wood. "Understanding, Humility, and the Vices of Pride." In *The Routledge Handbook of Virtue Epistemology*, edited by Heather Battaly, 363–75. Routledge Handbooks of Philosophy. London: Routledge, 2019.

BIBLIOGRAPHY

Adams, Robert Merrihew. *A Theory of Virtue: Excellence in Being for the Good.* New York: Oxford University Press, 2006.

Anscombe, Elizabeth. "Modern Moral Philosophy." *Philosophy* 33 (1958) 1–19.

Aristotle. *Nicomachean Ethics.* Translated with an introduction by David Ross, revised by J. L. Ackrill and J. O. Urmson. Oxford: Oxford University Press, 1998.

———. *Politics.* Translated by C. D. C. Reeve. Indianapolis: Hackett, 1998.

Emerson, Ralph Waldo. "Gifts." Blupete, 1844. http://www.blupete.com/Literature/Essays/Best/EmersonGifts.htm.

Greenspan, Patricia S. *Emotions & Reasons: An Inquiry into Emotional Justification.* London: Routledge, 2014.

Held, Shai. *Judaism Is about Love.* New York: Farrar, Straus, and Giroux, 2024.

Hume, David. *Treatise of Human Nature.* Edited by David Fate Norton and Mary J. Norton. Oxford Philosophical Texts. 1888. Oxford: Oxford University Press, 2000.

Hursthouse, Rosalind. *On Virtue Ethics.* Oxford: Oxford University Press, 1999.

Kant, Immanuel. *Groundwork of the Metaphysics of Morals.* Various editions. 1785.

MacIntyre, Alasdair. *After Virtue: A Study in Moral Theory.* Notre Dame, IN: University of Notre Dame Press, 1981.

McGraw, Phillip C. "Dr. Phil's Ten Life Laws." Dr. Phil, May 25, 2023. https://www.drphil.com/advice/dr-phils-ten-life-laws.

Mill, John Stuart. *Utilitarianism.* Gutenberg, 1861. https://www.gutenberg.org/ebooks/11224.

Nash, Ogden. "Kind of an Ode to Beauty." Poetry Nook, n.d. https://www.poetrynook.com/poem/kind-ode-duty.

Nussbaum, Martha. *Upheavals of Thought: The Intelligence of Emotions.* Princeton, NJ: Princeton University Press, 2001.

Plato. *Complete Works.* Edited by John M. Cooper and D. S. Hutchinson. Indianapolis: Hackett, 1997.

Rawls, John. *A Theory of Justice.* Cambridge: Harvard University Press, 1971.

Ryle, Gilbert. *The Concept of Mind.* London: Hutchinson, 1949.

"Surfside Condominium Collapse." Wikipedia, last edited Oct. 20, 2024. https://en.wikipedia.org/wiki/Surfside_condominium_collapse.

Taylor, Jessica. "Comey: Trump Asked for 'Loyalty,' Wanted Him to 'Let' Flynn Investigation 'Go.'" NPR, June 7, 2017. https://www.npr.org/2017/06/07/531927032/comey-trump-asked-for-loyalty-wanted-him-to-let-flynn-investigation-go.

Watson, Gary. "On the Primacy of Virtue." In *Identity, Character, and Morality: Essays in Moral Psychology*, edited by Owen Flanagan and Amélie Oksenberg Rorty, 449–69. Cambridge: MIT Press, 1993.

Whitcomb, Dennis, et al. "Intellectual Humility: Owning Our Limitations." *Philosophy and Phenomenological Research* 94 (2017) 509–39. https://doi.org/10.1111/phpr.12228.

Wolterstorff, Nicholas. *Justice: Rights and Wrongs.* Princeton, NJ: Princeton University Press, 2008.

www.ingramcontent.com/pod-product-compliance
Lightning Source LLC
Chambersburg PA
CBHW030111170426
43198CB00009B/574